SRA
Open Court Reading **Skills Practice**

BOOK 1

Grade 5

McGraw Hill Education

mheducation.com/prek-12

Send all inquiries to:
McGraw-Hill Education
8787 Orion Place
Columbus, OH 43240

ISBN: 978-0-07-900021-7
MHID: 0-07-900021-5

Printed in the United States of America

9 10 11 12 13 BRR 26 25 24 23 A

Table of Contents

Prefixes *non-, pre-*; Suffixes *-ness, -ment*

FOCUS The prefix *non-* means "not." Adding *non-* to a root or base word creates an antonym, or a word with the opposite meaning.

The prefix *pre-* means "before."

The suffix *-ness* means "state of being" or "condition of." Adding *-ness* to an adjective creates a noun.

The suffix *-ment* means "action" or "process." Adding *-ment* to an adjective or verb changes it into a noun.

PRACTICE Add *non-, pre-, -ness,* or *-ment* to each base word below to create a real word. Then write the new word's definition on the line. Use a dictionary if you need help.

1. _____poisonous

   _____

2. _____order

   _____

3. arrange_____

   _____

4. clever_____

   _____

5. achieve_____

   _____

APPLY Each word contains the prefix *non-*, the prefix *pre-*, the suffix *-ness*, or the suffix *-ment*. Choose the word that best fits the definition and use it in a sentence.

| amusement | assortment | brightness | fairness |
| nonemergency | nonfiction | preseason | preplan |

6. action of assorting _____

_____

7. not fiction _____

_____

8. state of being fair _____

_____

9. plan before _____

_____

10. action of amusing _____

_____

11. not an emergency _____

_____

12. before the season _____

_____

Vocabulary

FOCUS Review the selection vocabulary words from "The Marble Champ."

association	nerves
chanced	privacy
commotion	quivering
fumed	reluctantly
glumly	rummaged
instinct	slate

PRACTICE Read each sentence. Think about the meaning of the underlined word or words. Write the vocabulary word on the line that is similar in meaning.

1. The athletic <u>organization</u> in our town plans tournaments. _____

2. It was hard to see the <u>dark gray</u> bird by the stone. _____

3. The student <u>searched</u> in his backpack for his homework. _____

4. The customer <u>was angry</u> when the product did not work. _____

5. The <u>disturbance</u> outside interrupted my quiet time. _____

6. I saw a scared, lost cat <u>shaking slightly</u> under a bush. _____

7. The child watched <u>unhappily</u> as the children played. _____

8. He <u>unwillingly</u> went to the poetry reading. _____

9. She needed <u>to be alone</u> when she wrote in her diary. _____

10. The young actor hoped his <u>nervousness</u> would not show. _____

11. By <u>acting without thinking</u>, the cat caught the mouse. _____

12. They <u>risked</u> being late when they stopped on the way. _____

APPLY Read each question. Think about the meaning of the underlined vocabulary word. Write your answers on the lines.

13. What would you make the color <u>slate</u> in a painting? _____

_____

14. What is something you do by <u>instinct</u>? _____

_____

15. What is something you do <u>reluctantly</u>? _____

_____

16. What might create a <u>commotion</u> in your community? _____

_____

17. When have you <u>rummaged</u> for something? _____

_____

18. What <u>association</u> helps the most in your school or neighborhood? _____

_____

Physical Chess

Now that he was in fifth grade, William wanted to find a sport that he could do well. He liked to think about strategy and work his muscles. He played some team sports in second and third grade. However, he had a hard time mastering the skills as quickly as the other kids on his team.

At first, he tried basketball, but he could never figure out how to dribble and run. He could do one or the other, but both seemed impossible, no matter how much he practiced. He was fuming when the referee blew the whistle every time he dribbled the ball. Each time the whistle sounded, he got more and more frustrated. After the game, he asked to be alone to think in private.

As he was thinking, he heard a series of commotions outside. He looked out the window to see a group of kids playing soccer. They worked together to move the ball down the field. When a team made a goal, they all cheered and yelled. It looked like fun, so he asked his parents if he could sign up for a local soccer team. Soon he was kicking a ball down the field with his new teammates.

As much as he loved playing outside and thinking about strategy, his instincts for soccer were terrible. He often missed open shots and could not get the ball to move where he wanted it to go. Many of his teammates had similar problems. His team lost every soccer game that season. He hung his head looking glum all the way home. When would he find a sport that he could do well?

Over the next week, William decided to play some strategy games. He rummaged through the closet looking for pieces to his favorite game: chess. He loved the challenge of the game. He would play with his older brother, his cousin, and his uncle. He tested new strategies in each game he played. "Why can't sports be like chess?" thought William.

William's mother knew how much he wanted to play a sport. At the local recreation center, she spotted a flyer on the wall. The local fencing association offered a beginning fencing class starting next week. It described fencing as "physical chess." This sounded like the perfect sport for William, but would he chance trying another sport?

William was reluctant to try a new sport, but the idea of "physical chess" intrigued him. He had to at least try the beginner class, and see if it would be a good fit. When he arrived at the fencing facility, he looked over the large, open room lined with slate mats. He watched as the fencers, covered with masks and special protective outfits, lunged and retreated in friendly matches. He heard buzzing and screams of triumph when one fencer got a point.

Coach Isabel introduced herself to the class, and then described all the equipment—William was most interested in the three different types of weapons. The first was an epee, which was the longest of the three weapons and the heaviest to use. The second was a foil, which was a shorter in length and lighter to hold. The third weapon was a saber. It was also short and light like the foil, but it had a curved metal piece around the hand guard.

Coach Isabel then described the basic differences of scoring for each weapon. To score a point with foil, fencers must touch only the chest, back, or mid-section of their opponent. To score a point with saber, fencers must touch their opponent above the waist; this includes arms and head! To score a point with epee, fencers must touch first— anywhere on the body!

Coach Isabel divided the class into two groups, directing one group to one side of the room, and the other group to the opposite side. She placed a glove in the middle. Each group had to work together to get the glove and move it to the opposite wall to score a point. William's nervousness evaporated as he began to strategize with his new teammates.

At the end of class, they tried the different weapons. William picked up the saber and practiced the slashing moves, but it did not feel quite right to him. Next, he tried the foil. It was also light but the action seemed too flimsy. Finally, he tried the epee—the long, heavy weapon. It was hard to hold for a long period of time, but he loved the way his muscles quivered and ached as he tried the different moves and techniques. He finally found the perfect sport to test his mind and body!

Apply Vocabulary • *Skills Practice 1*

Making Inferences

FOCUS Readers get clues from the text and use their own prior knowledge to **make inferences** about characters and events in a story.

PRACTICE Read each sentence below. Make an inference about the character based on each sentence and write it on the line.

1. Jordan saw the bus and quickly put on his coat, grabbed his book bag, and raced outside.

   Inference: _____

2. Mia thought about horses constantly, reading books and drawing pictures of them.

   Inference: _____

3. Ethan breathed heavily, holding back tears as he finished the race.

   Inference: _____

APPLY **Read the description of each character below. Then write a short paragraph describing how the character feels without actually stating it.**

4. a father who is proud about his child

_____

_____

_____

_____

5. an athlete who is confident

_____

_____

_____

_____

6. a neighbor who is unfriendly

_____

_____

_____

_____

Access Complex Text • ***Skills Practice 1***

Name _____ **Date** _____

Opinion Writing

Think

Audience: Who will read your opinion essay?

_____

Purpose: What is your reason for writing an opinion essay?

_____

PREWRITING Write the topic you have chosen in the center space. Generate opinions related to the topic, and write them in the surrounding areas.

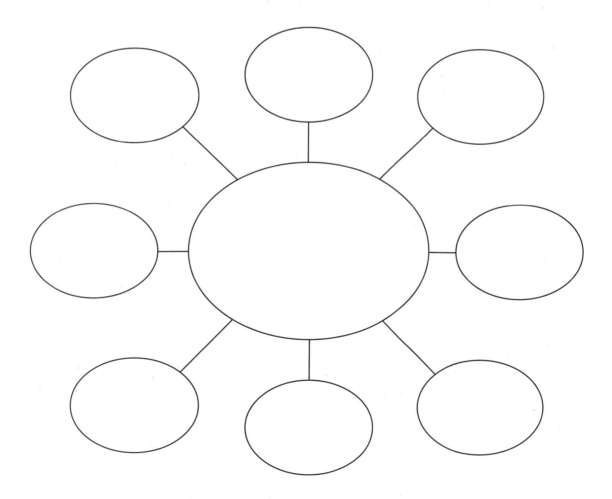

Revising

Use this checklist to revise your opinion essay.

☐ Does your writing have an introduction that states an opinion?

☐ Does your writing have reasons that support your opinion?

☐ Are your reasons presented in an order that makes sense?

☐ Did you include a conclusion that sums up your opinion?

☐ Does your writing include transition words?

☐ Does your writing have a clear purpose?

Editing/Proofreading

Use this checklist to correct mistakes in your opinion essay.

☐ Did you use proofreading symbols when editing?

☐ Did you check your writing for mistakes in nouns, pronouns, and verbs?

☐ Did you check your writing for spelling mistakes?

Publishing

Use this checklist to prepare your opinion writing for publishing.

☐ Write or type a neat copy of your opinion writing.

☐ Add a photograph or a drawing.

Prefixes *non-* and *pre-* and Suffixes *-ness* and *-ment*

FOCUS
- The **prefix *non-*** usually means "not."
- The **prefix *pre-*** means "before."
- The **suffix *-ness*** means "the state or quality of." Words with this suffix are nouns.
- The **suffix *-ment*** means "an action or process." It is added to verbs to form nouns.

PRACTICE Add a prefix or suffix to each base word as indicated.

Word List
1. arrangement
2. contentment
3. endorsement
4. fondness
5. forgiveness
6. generousness
7. government
8. improvement
9. loneliness
10. nastiness
11. nonabsorbent
12. nondescript
13. nonexistent
14. nonresponsive
15. nontoxic
16. prearrange
17. precaution
18. predawn
19. prehistoric
20. preseason

Challenge Words
1. nonabrasive
2. predetermine
3. queasiness

Add the prefix *non-*.

1. toxic _____

2. descript _____

3. existent _____

Add the prefix *pre-*.

4. dawn _____

5. historic _____

6. arrange _____

Add the suffix *-ness*.

7. generous _____

8. lonely _____

9. fond _____

Add the suffix *-ment*.

10. improve _____

11. content _____

12. govern _____

APPLY Write the spelling word that matches each definition on the line.

13. be careful ahead of time _____

14. affection for something _____

15. the action of making something better _____

16. the state of feeling sick or dizzy _____

17. sadness about being alone _____

18. the action of governing _____

19. not poisonous or harmful _____

20. the action of feeling satisfied _____

21. not existing in real life _____

22. does not hold moisture _____

23. the act of approval and support _____

24. the act of forgiving _____

25. plan beforehand _____

26. before the sun comes up _____

27. the quality of being kind and giving _____

28. does not react _____

29. the quality of being unkind and mean _____

30. the process of planning _____

Spelling • *Skills Practice 1*

Nouns and Pronouns

FOCUS Nouns name people, places, things, or ideas.
- A **common noun** is used to name a general, or nonspecific, person, place, or thing.

  teacher, library, books
- A **proper noun** is used to name a particular, or specific person, place, or thing.

  Ms. Yukiko, New York City
- **Concrete nouns** name people, places, and things that can be sensed (seen, touched, heard). The examples above are all concrete nouns.
- **Abstract nouns** name ideas, qualities, or feelings that cannot be sensed.

  love, time, awareness

A **pronoun** can take the place of a noun in a sentence.
- A **subject pronoun** replaces one or more nouns in the subject.

  Max ran quickly and won the race.
  He ran quickly and won the race.
- An **object pronoun** replaces one or more nouns in the predicate.

  The teacher smiled at **the students**.
  The teacher smiled at **them**.

PRACTICE Circle the nouns and pronouns in the following sentences.

1. Ellis Island opened in 1892 as an immigration station in New York.

2. Immigrants arrived from countries such as Germany, Ireland, Turkey, Poland, and Greece.

3. It was hard for them to leave home, but the United States held the promise of a brighter future.

4. If you have a chance to visit the Ellis Island Immigration Museum, you will learn about the history of millions of Americans and the new lives they hoped to begin.

APPLY Rewrite each sentence so that the underlined noun (or nouns) are replaced by a pronoun.

5. <u>Erika's</u> book report was due on Tuesday.

_____

6. Erika anxiously stood up when <u>Micah and Li</u> had finished.

_____

7. She focused her attention on <u>the book</u>.

_____

Read the following paragraph. Write C over each common noun. Write P over each proper noun.

The pink river dolphin makes its home in the Amazon River. It is found in several countries of South America, including Brazil, Ecuador, and Colombia. Unlike most other dolphins, it lives only in freshwater. Organizations like the World Wildlife Fund are working to make sure that this unique creature is protected from threats such as fishermen and pollution.

Read the following paragraph. Circle each abstract noun.

Last year, my sister Isabel started a group to raise money for homeless pets. I admire her determination and generosity. Isabel has always loved animals, so she decided to use her creativity to figure out how to help them. Her sympathy for animals in trouble and her excitement for this cause are an inspiration to me. Isabel has great pride in her work. She takes satisfaction in knowing that she is making a difference in the world.

Latin Roots *loc, flect,* Greek Roots *cycl, phon*

FOCUS Greek and Latin roots are common in the English language. Identifying and understanding roots can help you define difficult and unfamiliar words. When you know the meaning of a root, you can determine the meanings of many words that contain that root.

The Greek root *loc* means "place." For example, the word *location* means "a place." The Greek root *flect* means "bend." For example, the word *reflect* means "to bend back."

The Latin root *cycl* means "circle" or "ring." For example, the word *cycle* means "circle" or "ring." The Latin root *phon* means "sound." For example, the word *telephone* means "a device that transmits sound."

PRACTICE Think of a word that uses each Greek or Latin root given below. Write the word on the line, and then use it in a sentence.

1. *loc* means "place" _____

_____

2. *flect* means "bend" _____

_____

3. *cycl* means "circle" or "ring" _____

_____

4. *phon* means "sound" _____

_____

APPLY Select the word with a Greek or Latin root that best fits the definition and write it on the line. Then use each word in a sentence.

allocate	earphones	flexible	locomotion
reflecting	recycle	saxophone	tricycle

5. Device worn over the ears that transmits sound _____

_____

6. Bending back _____

_____

7. To set aside for something specific _____

_____

8. Something that is able to be bent _____

_____

9. A vehicle with three wheels _____

_____

10. The act of moving from place to place _____

_____

11. A musical instrument with a metal tube that is curved and was invented by

Antoine Sax _____

_____

12. To use again _____

_____

Word Analysis • *Skills Practice 1*

Vocabulary

FOCUS Review the selection vocabulary words from "Queen of the Track."

anonymous	relays
athletics	rescue worker
campus	segregation
clear	toll
dainty	tuition
hardships	vaulted
proclaimed	

PRACTICE Complete each sentence with a selection vocabulary word. Each vocabulary word should be used once.

1. Choosing a book is the first obstacle to _____ for writing a book report.

2. The high jumper _____ over the bar with inches to spare.

3. A(n) _____ helped the family after the flood caused water to fill their home.

4. The announcer _____ the winner over the speaker.

5. The _____ donor did not want to be recognized at the opening of the community center.

6. The swimmers competed in _____ after their individual races.

7. Football, basketball, baseball, softball, and track are all part of the _____ department.

8. Because of _____, the athletes were separated by race into different leagues.

9. The college was a small _____ with few buildings, an athletic center, and a student center.

10. The _____ young woman greeted the guest politely with a soft, delicate handshake.

11. The student encountered many _____ including illness and limited resources.

12. The many hours of practice had taken a(n) _____ on the athlete's body.

13. The cost of _____ was paid by a scholarship as long as the student had good grades.

APPLY Read each sentence. Answer each question by explaining the definition in your own words.

14. A <u>rescue worker</u> shows up to help after a hurricane. What might he do?

_____

15. The team <u>relays</u> are the last events of the night. How do they work?

_____

16. You are taking a tour of a <u>campus</u> in a small city. Where are you?

_____

17. The judges <u>proclaimed</u> a winner of the writing contest. What has happened?

_____

18. The <u>tuition</u> will go up this year. How does this affect students?

_____

Practice Vocabulary • *Skills Practice 1*

Living History

Before the class got on the bus for their field trip to the Senior Center, Mrs. Howard explained the purpose for the visit. "We are starting a new history unit, and I want to you to ask the residents of the Senior Center some good questions. Pairs of students will be partnered with a resident. Later, you will introduce your resident to the group." After that brief introduction, Mrs. Howard's class brainstormed questions and decided on the top three to ask during their visits. Mrs. Howard reminded her students, "Remember, the daintiest lady may have the most interesting and exciting life story—you never know until you ask." After a short bus ride, the class arrived at the Senior Center campus, and Mrs. Howard introduced the students to their senior neighbors. She reminded the students to be polite and to use their good listening skills.

Sophie and Ashley met Mrs. Chen, who was daintily drinking a cup of tea. They remembered what Mrs. Howard said, so they started, "Good morning, Mrs. Chen. We are here today to ask about some of your life stories. Did you have any interesting jobs when you were younger?" Mrs. Chen smiled at the girls and began to tell her story, which was full of excitement and heartache.

Jayden and Daniel met Mr. Johnson, who was a tall fellow leaning back in his chair, stretching his long legs. The boys looked over their questions, and then asked, "Mr. Johnson, what job did you have that you were proudest of?" Mr. Johnson answered almost immediately, but with a short response. Jayden and Daniel knew they needed more information, so they asked some follow-up questions, and soon Mr. Johnson was describing all different parts of his job.

Maddie and Emily met Mrs. Garcia, who greeted them with a warm smile and a surprisingly low voice. The girls soon found out that Mrs. Garcia had a job they never knew existed, so they vaulted right into many follow-up questions to learn more about her and her job.

The students listened carefully as their senior partners described their jobs, some of their life stories, including a hardship or two. The students wanted to learn more about any experiences with segregation, as well as experiences that took a toll on them. Mrs. Howard asked her class and the senior residents to wrap up their discussions so the students could introduce their senior neighbors to the group. Students rewrote their notes so they could present about their assigned seniors.

After a few minutes, Mrs. Howard called on Sophie and Ashley to begin. Sophie announced to the group, "This is Mrs. Chen. She has been a resident of our town for seventy years, but has traveled all over the world doing a very special job."

"Mrs. Chen was a director at the American Red Cross," continued Ashley. "She coordinated rescue workers after natural disasters like hurricanes or tornados."

"Thank you, Sophie and Ashley," said Mrs. Howard. "Jayden and Daniel, who did you meet?"

Jayden stood up and stretched his arm to make his introduction. "This is Mr. Johnson. He was an assistant director of athletics at the local college."

"He helped student athletes apply for scholarships to pay for their tuition," said Daniel, "and he planned athletic events on campus throughout the year for all students."

Mr. Johnson added, "and I use those same skills to create relay races here at the senior center from time to time. Maybe we could try one before you leave!" The class cheered at that suggestion.

"That's a generous offer, Mr. Johnson," said Mrs. Howard. "We might not have enough time. We do have a bus to catch! Let's hear from Maddie and Emily."

Maddie stood up next to Mrs. Garcia and spoke slowly in a loud voice, "This is Mrs. Garcia. She is a self-proclaimed life coach. You might ask yourself what a self-proclaimed life coach is because we did."

Emily continued, "Well, a life coach is someone who helps people set goals and clear any hurdles that get in the way of those goals. She helps people find a balance between working hard and enjoying life. She did not go to school or receive special training. Do you want to know the best part of her job?"

"She coached several famous people," answered Maddie as Mrs. Garcia nodded. "But she refused to tell us their names because she promised that they would remain anonymous."

"It is time to head back to school," said Mrs. Howard. "Let's thank our new friends and wish them well."

Copyright © McGraw-Hill Education

Apply Vocabulary • *Skills Practice 1*

Sequence

> **FOCUS** The **sequence** in which events occur in a story is indicated by time words and order words.

PRACTICE Read each sentence. Write the time and order word or phrase in each sentence on the line.

1. We planted flower bulbs in the fall last year.

   _____

2. This spring, the colorful flowers bloomed in the side garden.

   _____

3. The athlete drank water and rested after the race.

   _____

4. On the Fourth of July, we will march in the Independence Day Parade.

   _____

5. Before school, I placed my packed lunch in my book bag.

   _____

6. My sister turns six years old in November.

   _____

7. She walks one mile every day, even in cold weather!

   _____

8. The final step of the writing process is publishing.

   _____

APPLY Read each paragraph below. Then, rewrite the events in the paragraph in the correct sequence.

9. We pick the vegetables at the end of summer. Every year we plant a garden. We water and weed the garden while the young plants grow. In the autumn, we freeze any leftover harvest. In the spring, we plant the seeds in the ground.

_____

_____

_____

_____

10. Next, place the kernels in a hot air popper. Popcorn is an easy snack to make. Finally, the popcorn pops into a snack. First, measure out the popcorn kernels. Then, turn on the popper so it heats the kernels.

_____

_____

_____

_____

Access Complex Text • *Skills Practice 1*

Opinion Writing

Think

Audience: Who will read your opinion essay?

_____

_____

Purpose: What is your reason for writing an opinion essay?

_____

_____

PREWRITING **It is important to think about the best order in which to present the reasons that support an opinion. Often the best approach is to order them from most important to least important. Sometimes one reason leads to a second or third related reason.**

Look at each set of three reasons supporting an opinion. Think about the most logical order in which they should be presented. Then write *1, 2,* and *3* on the lines to show the order.

1. Cell phones should not be allowed in schools.

    _____ Kids already spend too much time using screens every day.

    _____ Cell phones at school distract from schoolwork.

    _____ Not all kids have phones, so some kids will feel left out.

2. Students should get paid for good grades.

    _____ Kids don't have many ways to earn money.

    _____ Hard work should be rewarded.

    _____ Everyone works harder when they are motivated.

Proofreading Symbols

¶   Indent the paragraph.

∧   Add something.

℘   Take out something.

/   Make a small letter.

☰   Make a capital letter.

sp   Check spelling.

⊙   Add a period.

Latin Roots *loc* and *flect* and
Greek Roots *cycl* and *phon*

FOCUS Understanding and identifying **Latin and Greek roots** and their meanings can help you define and spell difficult and unfamiliar words. Here are the roots in the spelling words and their meanings:

Latin roots: **loc** = "place"; **flect** = "bend"

Greek roots: **cycl** = "circle"; **phon** = "sound"

PRACTICE Fill in the appropriate Latin or Greek root to create a spelling word.

Word List		Challenge Words
1. allocate	**11.** locomotive	**1.** antireflective
2. cyclist	**12.** motorcycle	**2.** cyclical
3. cyclops	**13.** phonetic	**3.** echolocation
4. deflect	**14.** phonics	
5. dislocate	**15.** phonograph	
6. encyclopedia	**16.** reflection	
7. genuflect	**17.** reflector	
8. inflection	**18.** saxophone	
9. locale	**19.** unicycle	
10. location	**20.** xylophone	

1. _____ics

2. uni_____e

3. _____ograph

4. de_____

5. _____omotive

6. xylo_____e

7. _____ale

8. in_____ion

9. _____etic

10. re_____or

11. genu_____

12. motor_____e

13. _____ist

14. en_____opedia

15. al_____ate

16. re_____ion

17. _____ops

18. saxo_____e

19. dis_____ate

20. _____ation

APPLY If the word is misspelled, write the correct spelling on the line. If the word is spelled correctly, write *Correct* on the line.

21. saxaphone _____

22. reflecter _____

23. cyclest _____

24. localle _____

25. echolocation _____

26. motorcicle _____

27. dislocate _____

28. phonigraph _____

29. genuflec _____

30. allacate _____

31. locimotive _____

32. unicycel _____

33. encyclopedia _____

34. ciclycal _____

Verbs

FOCUS Verbs are words that show action or express a state of being.

- **Action verbs** describe an action.

  Malcolm **grew** tomatoes and peppers.

- **State-of-being** verbs express a condition of existence. They are often forms of the verb *be*, such as *is, are, was, were,* and *am*. The verbs *feel, smell, appear, seem,* and *taste* can also be used as state-of-being verbs.

  Tomorrow **is** the last day of school.

- A **verb phrase** consists of one or more helping verbs used with an action or state-of-being verb.

  I **have picked** a book for my report. She **might be** worried about the performance this weekend.

- The **active voice** of a verb is used when the subject is performing the action. The **passive voice** of a verb is used when the subject receives the verb's action.

  Passive: The **kite was flown** by Darius. Active: **Darius flew** the kite.

PRACTICE In the following sentences, circle the verb or verb phrase. Then write A on the line if the main verb is an action verb. Write S if it is a state-of-being verb.

1. Natalie waited inside the cab. _____

2. Sometimes our garbage smells like rotten eggs. _____

3. Next year I will read *Tom Sawyer*. _____

4. The astronauts could see Earth from outer space. _____

5. The pitcher threw the batter a curve ball. _____

6. Apples and olives taste terrible together. _____

APPLY Rewrite the sentences below from the passive voice to the active voice.

7. The radio was being listened to by me. _____

_____

_____

8. I am being ignored by everyone who walks in here. _____

_____

_____

9. Some of the clothes are made by them. _____

_____

_____

10. The business will be inherited by him. _____

_____

_____

11. The pitas are carried by my mom. _____

_____

_____

12. The door is being painted by Sam. _____

_____

_____

Grammar • *Skills Practice 1*

Suffixes *-ize, -ance/-ence*

FOCUS The suffix *-ize* means "to make." Adding *-ize* to adjectives and nouns forms verbs. For example, adding *-ize* to the adjective *vocal* changes it to *vocalize,* which means "to make vocal."

The suffix *-ance/-ence* means "state of" or "quality of." Adding *-ance/-ence* to adjectives and verbs forms nouns. For example, *resistance* means "state of resisting" and *obedience* means "state of being obedient."

PRACTICE Read each sentence. The boldfaced word contains a suffix taught in this lesson. On the line, write *N* if the word is a noun or *V* if the word is a verb.

1. _____ The school was honored for teaching **excellence** in the city.

2. _____ The puppy bears a **resemblance** to the missing one shown online.

3. _____ The cyclist was **hospitalized** after the accident.

4. _____ During dance class today, we will practice **synchronizing** our steps.

5. _____ The **fragrance** of the flowers filled the room.

6. _____ The test indicates the child has high **intelligence.**

7. _____ The doctor needs to **authorize** an appointment with the specialist.

8. _____ Do you **recognize** any of the items in the lost and found?

APPLY Complete the "word-math" problems below by combining the base word and suffix and writing the word on the line. Then use each word in a sentence.

9. familiar + ize = _____

_____

_____

10. exist + ence = _____

_____

_____

11. attend + ance = _____

_____

_____

12. public + ize = _____

_____

_____

13. enter + ance = _____

_____

_____

14. prefer + ence = _____

_____

_____

Word Analysis • *Skills Practice 1*

Vocabulary

> **FOCUS** Review the selection vocabulary words from "One Small Step."

awry	magnitude
capsule	onboard
descending	rendezvoused
esteemed	resounding
fatigue	thrusters
glitches	ventures

PRACTICE Read each sentence. Write the vocabulary word on the line that best completes each sentence.

1. If someone ran a marathon, that person would likely feel much _____.

2. When the astronaut worked on the rocket engines, she fixed the

   _____.

3. If your plans were changed unexpectedly, they went _____.

4. When you walk down a set of stairs, you are _____.

5. If the car has a mapping system installed in it, the system is _____.

6. The class put items for a future class in a time _____.

7. It was frustrating to work on the computer program with so many

_____.

8. This new treatment is a medical advancement of great _____.

9. The scientist won many awards and was highly _____.

10. Some people consider parachuting and bungee jumping to be big

_____.

11. The approval and support for the new community park was _____.

12. The two friends played separately and then near the end of recess they

_____.

APPLY Read each question. Think about the meaning of the underlined vocabulary word. Write your answers on the line.

13. What might cause someone to feel <u>fatigue</u>? _____

14. Who is an <u>esteemed</u> scientist you know of? _____

15. How would you know if you had <u>resounding</u> support for a project?

_____

16. What <u>ventures</u> are the most dangerous? _____

17. When have you had plans that went <u>awry</u>? _____

18. Where have you <u>rendezvoused</u> with friends? _____

New Space Ventures

"Matthew," called Mom, "I need you to entertain your little sister while I make dinner."

Matthew tried looking fatigued and replied, "But Mom, I've had a long day at school. I don't think I could keep her busy that long!"

"I am sure you will think of something," she answered. "Mia holds you in high esteem."

"I know *Mia* will think of something," thought Matthew. His sister was six years old with a magnitude of ideas. Currently, Mia wanted to learn all about space and astronauts. So, he and his family had read several books to her about Sally Ride and Mae Jemison. Maybe he *could* think of something this time.

Matthew saw Mia sitting on the sofa reading one of the space books from the library. He got closer and pretended to talk into a communication device, saying "Mia…let's rendezvous at the space headquarters in T-minus four minutes. Over."

Mia looked up at her brother, ready to play along. She glanced around the room, peeking over her book, and answered into her imaginary communication device, "Roger." Mia resoundingly loved the official sound of "Roger" to say "Okay" when they played this game. She and her brother walked all over the house sneakily, in opposite directions, to make sure they were not followed.

Four minutes later, Mia peeked into her brother's room. It was covered with posters and models of space. A large poster showing a space capsule floating in space was in the center. Drawings of planets, both real and imaginary, decorated the wall around it. Models of other spacecrafts waited on his bookshelves for future missions, while planets dangled on string from his ceiling. She knocked on the door with three quick taps and entered saying, "Reporting for duty, sir."

"Thank you, Mia. I hope you will accept this next venture that I have for you. It will not be easy, but I know you are the person for the job. The right thruster is not working properly, and it needs to be adjusted before the next crew can go into space. They are counting on you to make everything work smoothly. Do you think you can fix it?" Matthew looked with great seriousness for Mia's reply.

"Of course!" she beamed, and then returned the serious tone, "Let me get my tools and get to work!"

Mia grabbed an imaginary toolbox and set to work on the right thruster, which looked a lot like a trash can on its side next to Matthew's bed. She pulled different tools out and tinkered on the part, stopping occasionally to wipe sweat off her brow and continue to work. Finally, she looked at her work with approval and declared, "Good as new."

"Great work, Mia," Matthew said as he thought, "Well that didn't take long. Now what will we do?"

"Thank you," replied Mia. "What do you say we take a ride in the shuttle? I know exactly where we can go to explore a new world!"

"That might be a good idea. Then we can make sure the glitch is fixed and the right thruster won't give our astronauts any problems," said Matthew, playing along. "Does this mean you will be the pilot?"

"Of course," she said confidently, as if she believed no one else in the room was qualified to be the pilot. Matthew and Mia sat in chairs next to each other. Matthew handed Mia a set of headphones to put on and he also put on a set so they could talk to each other during the flight. Mia made sure they both buckled up and then she checked on the onboard switches. She flipped imaginary switches up and down, and finally asked her brother, "Ready?"

Matthew nodded and up they went, blasting through the atmosphere and soon looking back at Earth. Mia shook the controls as they headed into space, and then smoothed her motions. She steered to the left, and Matthew leaned to the left. Then, she steered to the right and Matthew leaned to the right. He finally commented, "I think it is working. I suppose we can head back now." Then, Matthew made a beeping sound and said in a panicked voice, "I think something is awry! What should we do?"

"Calm down," Mia responded. "I will just drive over to the space station. They have some extra tools and they know tons about rockets and space." Mia steered to the left and then to the right, and finally she pulled down on the steering to make it go down.

"Don't descend too quickly or we will be in trouble!" said Matthew.

"I know what I'm doing, so just hold on while I slow this thing down," said Mia.

Matthew heard the final sound of the mission: his mother calling from the kitchen, "Dinner!"

Apply Vocabulary • *Skills Practice 1*

Classifying and Categorizing

FOCUS
- **Classifying** is identifying the similarities that objects, characters, or events have in common with each other, and then grouping them by their similarities.
- **Categorizing** is the act of organizing the objects, characters, or events into groups, or categories.

PRACTICE On the lines below, clothes will be categorized into tops and bottoms. Classify the items listed in the box by placing them into the appropriate category.

shirt	blouse	skirt	slacks
pants	shorts	sweater	jacket

1. **Tops**

_____

_____

_____

2. **Bottoms**

_____

_____

_____

APPLY Classify the types of travel listed in the box by placing them into their appropriate categories on the lines below.

boat	airplane	car	jet	ship	ocean liner
van	truck	yacht	glider	train	hot-air balloon

3. **By Land**

_____

_____

_____

4. **By Sea**

_____

_____

_____

5. **By Air**

_____

_____

_____

Access Complex Text • *Skills Practice 1*

Opinion Writing

Think

Audience: Who will read your opinion essay?

_____

Purpose: What is your reason for writing an opinion essay?

_____

PREWRITING **Brainstorm five possible opinions about a chosen topic. Record your ideas on the lines below.**

Topic: _____

Opinion #1: _____

_____

Opinion #2: _____

_____

Opinion #3: _____

_____

Opinion #4: _____

_____

Opinion #5: _____

_____

Revising

Use this checklist to revise your opinion essay.

☐ Does your writing have an introduction that states an opinion?

☐ Does your writing have reasons that support your opinion?

☐ Did you include a conclusion that sums up your opinion?

☐ Does your writing include transition words?

☐ Did you look for and replace overused words or phrases?

☐ Does your writing include detailed and descriptive language?

Editing/Proofreading

Use this checklist to correct mistakes in your opinion essay.

☐ Did you use proofreading symbols when editing?

☐ Did you check your writing for mistakes in adjectives and adverbs?

☐ Did you check your writing for spelling mistakes?

Publishing

Use this checklist to prepare your opinion writing for publishing.

☐ Write or type a neat copy of your opinion writing.

☐ Add a photograph or a drawing.

Suffixes *-ize* and *-ance/-ence*

> **FOCUS**
> - The **suffix *-ize*** means "to make." When it is added to a base word, it creates a verb.
> - The **suffix *-ance/-ence*** means "state or quality of." When it is added to a base word, it creates a noun.

PRACTICE On the line, write the spelling word with the suffix *-ize* that shares the same base word with the following words.

Word List		Challenge Words
1. abundance	11. ignorance	1. characterize
2. authorize	12. inheritance	2. correspondence
3. criticize	13. insurance	3. mesmerize
4. elegance	14. legalize	
5. emphasize	15. magnetize	
6. evidence	16. organize	
7. existence	17. preference	
8. fragrance	18. reference	
9. harmonize	19. specialize	
10. hypnotize	20. sterilize	

1. sterile _____

2. organ _____

3. magnetic _____

4. illegal _____

5. emphasis _____

6. hypnotic _____

7. specialist _____

8. harmonica _____

9. authority _____

10. critical _____

On the line, write the spelling word with the suffix *-ance/-ence* that shares the same base word with the following words.

11. referred _____

12. fragrant _____

13. insuring _____

14. inelegant _____

15. abundant _____

16. ignore _____

17. prefer _____   **19.** inheritor _____

18. evident _____   **20.** existed _____

APPLY Look at each underlined spelling word in the sentences. If it is spelled incorrectly, write the correct spelling on the line. If it is spelled correctly, write *Correct*.

21. The nurses must <u>sterlize</u> the surgical tools before they can be used again.

_____

22. Edie appreciated the swan's <u>elegence</u> as it floated proudly and gracefully

across the pond. _____

23. Our <u>insurence</u> for the boat needs to be renewed before the end of the month.

_____

24. The colorful, flashing lights of the fair's midway <u>mesmerize</u> me.

_____

25. The sweet <u>fragrense</u> of honeysuckle hangs over the meadow.

_____

26. Do you have any <u>evidence</u> that Finn took the last apple? _____

27. The house was filled with an <u>abundence</u> of joy when Ollie came home.

_____

28. I'm surprised that you believe in the <u>exsistance</u> of dragons. _____

29. Reading in bed is usually my <u>prefrence</u> for a Saturday night at home.

_____

30. Two restaurants near my house <u>specalize</u> in Italian dishes. _____

Adjectives and Adverbs

FOCUS **Adjectives** modify nouns.

- Adjectives show what kind, how many, and which one.

    colorful shirts; **several** children

- Proper adjectives are formed from proper nouns. They are almost always capitalized.

    French toast; **Jewish** deli

Adverbs modify verbs, adjectives, and other adverbs.

- Adverbs show how, when, where, and to what extent.

    walked **slowly**; bowled **yesterday**; jumping **around**; **very** quiet

PRACTICE **Circle the adjectives, and underline the adverbs in the following paragraph.**

Each spring, Washington, D. C. is filled with the colorful blossoms of Japanese cherry trees. In 1912, Tokyo's mayor generously donated three thousand trees. They clearly symbolized the growing friendship between Japan and America. A two-week festival is held annually to celebrate the blossoming trees and Japanese culture. In Japanese culture, the cherry tree represents many things. For example, during the time of the samurai, fallen blossoms from the cherry tree represented warriors who had died bravely in battle.

APPLY Read each numbered sentence. On the first line of each lettered sentence, write *adjective* or *adverb*. On the second line, write the word or phrase from the box that describes how the adjective or adverb functions in the sentence.

how	what kind	where	to what extent
when	how many	which one	

1. They **always** relaxed in Shane's **backyard** fort when it was too **hot** to play basketball.

   a. *Always* is an _____; it tells _____.

   b. *Backyard* is an _____; it tells _____.

   c. *Hot* is an _____; it tells _____.

2. **Suddenly**, a **loud** crash echoed through Shane's **normally** calm yard.

   a. *Suddenly* is an _____; it tells _____.

   b. *Loud* is an _____; it tells _____.

   c. *Normally* is an _____; it tells _____.

3. The **two** boys **quickly** ran **out** of the fort.

   a. *Two* is an _____; it tells _____.

   b. *Quickly* is an _____; it tells _____.

   c. *Out* is an _____; it tells _____.

4. A **massive** branch from an **English** oak tree had fallen.

   a. *Massive* is an _____; it tells _____.

   b. *English* is an _____; it tells _____.

Grammar • *Skills Practice 1*

Greek Roots *logos* and *graph*

FOCUS Identifying and understanding Greek roots can help you define difficult and unfamiliar words. When you know the meaning of a Greek root, you can determine the meanings of many words that contain that root.

The Greek root *log/logos* means "word," "saying," or "thought." For example, the word *apology* means "words to say one is sorry." The Greek root *graph* means "write." For example, the word *paragraph* means "a group of written sentences about one idea."

PRACTICE Read each word. Circle the Greek root *log/logos* or *graph* in each one. Then write the definition of the word on the line.

1. apologize

_____

2. choreographer

_____

3. logical

_____

4. homograph

_____

5. geography

_____

6. analogy

_____

APPLY Choose a word from the box to complete each sentence. Each word contains the Greek root *log/logos* or *graph*. Write the word on the line.

apology	autobiography	biography	dialogue
epilogue	graphic	logical	logogram

7. My mom had a(n) _____ with my teacher yesterday about my schoolwork and class participation.

8. After we read the story, we read the _____.

9. The website put up a new _____ that shows the results of the soccer tournament.

10. A _____ is a symbol that represents a word or a phrase.

11. My sister had a(n) _____ explanation for why she couldn't finish her chores.

12. Frederick Douglass wrote a(n) _____ of his life as a slave in America in the 1800s.

13. I gave my brother a(n) _____ for playing with his football without asking.

14. The next book I read is going to be a(n) _____ about Martin Luther King, Jr.

Word Analysis • *Skills Practice 1*

Vocabulary

FOCUS Review the selection vocabulary words from "The Great Serum Race."

eerie	quarantine
epidemic	serum
freight	symptoms
mushers	treacherous
perished	twilight
plight	wade

PRACTICE Read each question. Choose the vocabulary word that answers the question and write it on the line.

1. If a community has a struggle with getting water, do they have a <u>plight</u> or a <u>serum</u>?

   _____

2. If it is nighttime, but you can still see some daylight, is it <u>treacherous</u> or <u>twilight</u>?

   _____

3. If the fog sits over the land looking mysterious, does it look <u>eerie</u> or <u>epidemic</u>?

   _____

4. If a man walked through water knee-deep, did he <u>quarantine</u> or <u>wade</u>?

   _____

5. If a person shows signs of the chicken pox, does the doctor see <u>symptoms</u> or <u>mushers</u>?

   _____

6. If the chicken pox spreads to everyone in town, is it an <u>epidemic</u> or a <u>serum</u>?

   _____

7. If a steep, rocky, and uneven trail is slippery, is the path perished or treacherous?

_____

8. If a truck transports a full load of school supplies, does it carry serum or freight?

_____

9. If people must be separated to keep disease from spreading, are they in quarantine or plight?

_____

10. If people train dogs to carry freight, are they mushers or symptoms?

_____

11. If a herd of wild animals died in the severe weather, have they perished or caused an epidemic?

_____

12. If the doctor recommends a medicinal liquid to heal the illness, does she recommend a serum or freight?

_____

APPLY Read each sentence. Answer each question by explaining the definition in your own words.

13. You are watching the hiking guide wade through the slow-moving stream. What is he doing?

_____

_____

14. You are home at twilight looking up at the sky. What do you see?

_____

_____

Practice Vocabulary • *Skills Practice 1*

Writing a Mystery

After taking a creative writing class, Angela was excited to try to write her first mystery. She knew it would be a challenge to include suspense and surprise. When she found out the local bookstore was having a writing contest for mysteries, she jumped at the chance to get her thoughts down on paper.

She knew she would have to create an eerie setting, and the eerier, the better. She pictured a setting that screamed eeriness in her mind: *an old abandoned house surrounded by a dark and dense forest at twilight.* She thought, "maybe layers of fog could be floating above a nearby meadow and there could be howling in the distance, like a wolf calling to the moon." She could add some more details about the house later.

Next, she needed a character to come across the old abandoned house. Who should it be? Perhaps it would be a truck driver, who is stranded but needs to get his perishable freight delivered. Or, maybe, it could be a dog sled musher, who lost his dogs in the fog and now he hears the dogs howling along with the wolf. Angela could not decide, so she thought about using both characters in her story.

Angela considered the plight of her characters. What could their main problem be? How would it be solved? How could she add suspense and surprise? This part took a little more thought. Maybe an epidemic hit the area, like smallpox or the flu, although it would be more mysterious if the illness was unknown. The mysterious disease could be symptomless until it was too late. Angela liked that idea.

Angela thought about the action that would happen in her story, at the beginning, middle, and end. In the beginning, she could describe the truck driver and his problem hauling freight. After he gets stuck on a treacherous drive, he starts walking in search of help. He and the musher meet at the abandoned house, where there is a notice posted about the epidemic. They look around and try to find someone. "And then what? How should this story end?" wondered Angela. She had an idea and began writing:

Tom did not think his luck could get much worse when suddenly his drive became more treacherous with an icy fog drifting across the road. His truck rumbled to a stop, and it would not start.

Tom needed to get the perishable items, including serum, to the address he scribbled down earlier. He was so close, and the voice on the phone was so urgent. Now only a few rays of light shone on the horizon as twilight set in and an unsettling breeze made his skin bristle. Tom decided to walk the rest of the way and find the place before carrying any freight by hand.

At the same time, Charles was returning from making an urgent phone call for help. He was a dog sled musher, out running his dogs for a local race when he came upon a house. A doctor stood on the porch steps and called out to him. He said there were several people inside who had come down with a mysterious illness. The symptoms were like another disease he had treated with a special serum. He gave Charles a number and asked him to hurry to a phone and request the serum. There was no reception at the house, and the doctor needed to stay with the patients. Charles agreed and said he would return to let the doctor know when to expect the serum.

Tom saw the top of a chimney among the trees at the top of the hill, so he trudged ahead to the house. The old wooden house looked recently abandoned. It had a sign on the door that read "BEWARE: QUARANTINE IN EFFECT. DO NOT ENTER." Tom thought this must be the place, but he could not see inside or hear any sounds except the distant sounds of dogs. He knocked on the door, but no answer.

As Charles approached the house with his dogs, he did not see the doctor, but a man looking in the window of the house. He called out to the man, but just then the dogs let out a yip and ran in all different directions. He had to go find the dogs before the fog that surrounded the house reached him. He ran off near the stream, wading in the chilly water to gather three of the dogs. Stepping on the other side of the stream, the dogs huddled together, refusing to take one step closer to the house.

The hairs on Charles's arms prickled, and a feeling of unease settled on him. Just then, the man opened the door and became part of the mysterious fog!

Compare and Contrast

FOCUS
- When writers **compare,** they tell how things, ideas, events, or characters are alike.
- When writers **contrast,** they tell how things, ideas, events, or characters are different.

PRACTICE Read each sentence below. Decide if the sentence is showing a comparison or a contrast. Then, rewrite each sentence reflecting the other term.

1. Both Justin and Jada like to draw horses.

   _____

2. My father likes to play basketball, but I like to play soccer.

   _____

3. A mouse and a squirrel are both animals found in a forest.

   _____

4. Angela and Ashley are both ten years old.

   _____

5. My sister likes to play checkers, but I like to play chess.

   _____

6. David and Jason both finished the big project last week.

   _____

APPLY On the lines below, compare and contrast two things each about books and magazines.

7. **Compare:** _____

_____

_____

_____

_____

8. **Contrast:** _____

_____

_____

_____

_____

Opinion Writing

Think

Audience: Who will read your opinion essay?

_____

Purpose: What is your reason for writing an opinion essay?

_____

PREWRITING Write the opinion you have chosen in the center space. Think about reasons that support your opinion. Write them in the surrounding areas. Choose the three strongest reasons to use in your essay.

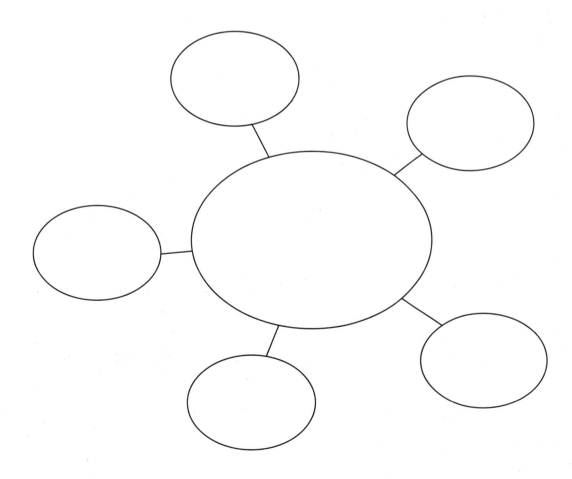

Revising

Use this checklist to revise your opinion essay.

☐ Does your writing have an effective introduction that catches the reader's attention?

☐ Is your opinion clearly stated in the introduction?

☐ Does your writing have three reasons that support your opinion?

☐ Does each reason have a further explanation?

☐ Did you use precise words?

☐ Does your writing include transition words and phrases?

☐ Does your writing have an effective conclusion that leaves the reader with a strong impression?

Editing/Proofreading

Use this checklist to correct mistakes in your opinion essay.

☐ Did you use proofreading symbols when editing?

☐ Did you check your writing for mistakes in nouns, pronouns, and verbs?

☐ Did you check your writing for direct objects to be sure they were used correctly?

☐ Did you check your writing for spelling mistakes?

Publishing

Use this checklist to prepare your opinion writing for publishing.

☐ Write or type a neat copy of your opinion writing.

☐ Add a photograph or a drawing.

Greek Roots *logos* and *graph*

FOCUS • Understanding and identifying Greek roots and their meanings can help you spell many new words. Here are the roots in the spelling words and their meanings:

logos/log = "word," "saying," or "thought"; *graph* = "write"

PRACTICE Fill in the root to create a spelling word. Use each spelling word only once.

Word List		Challenge Words
1. analogous	**11.** graphic	**1.** cartography
2. analogy	**12.** logical	**2.** epilogue
3. apologize	**13.** logistics	**3.** prologue
4. autobiography	**14.** logogram	
5. autograph	**15.** neologism	
6. calligraphy	**16.** paragraph	
7. catalog	**17.** photograph	
8. choreograph	**18.** seismograph	
9. chronological	**19.** slogan	
10. geography	**20.** telegraph	

1. photo + _____

2. neo + _____ + ism

3. calli + _____ + y

4. ana + _____ + ous

5. apo + _____ + ize

6. choreo + _____

7. para + _____

8. _____ + gram

9. chrono + _____ + ical

10. geo + _____ + y

11. autobio + _____ + y

12. ana + _____ + y

13. s + _____ + an

14. seismo + _____

15. cata + _____

16. _____ + ic

17. tele + _____

18. _____ + istics

19. auto + _____

20. _____ + ical

APPLY Choose the word that does not share the same main root as the other two and write it on the line.

21. geography, neologism, calligraphy   _____

22. slogan, autobiography, epilogue   _____

23. choreograph, chronological, analogy   _____

24. prologue, catalog, autograph   _____

25. analogous, autobiography, logistics   _____

26. seismograph, geography, apologize   _____

27. apologize, paragraph, logical   _____

28. graphic, photograph, slogan   _____

29. analogy, cartography, choreograph   _____

If the word is misspelled, write the correct spelling. If the spelling is correct, write *Correct*.

30. analogus   _____

31. caligriphy   _____

32. apalogize   _____

33. logical   _____

34. neolagism   _____

35. telegraf   _____

36. logoistics   _____

37. catalog   _____

38. photugraph   _____

39. autobigraffy   _____

40. chronelogicil   _____

Direct Objects

FOCUS
- A **direct object** is a noun or pronoun that receives the action of the verb.
  Mr. Thompson ran a **marathon** during the rain.
  The fire fighters sprayed **chemicals** onto the blaze.

- The direct object in a sentence can be identified by asking *what*? or *whom*? in a question with the verb.
  We will pick apples this fall. *Pick what?* **apples**
  Please drive Anna to her piano lesson this afternoon. *Drive whom?* **Anna**

PRACTICE Circle the direct objects in the sentences below. Some sentences have more than one direct object.

1. Al carried his pens and pencils in the front pocket of his backpack.

2. Kevin and Tyler climbed a ladder to get into the treehouse.

3. I poured cereal into the bowl and added dried blueberries.

4. The printer spit out a crumpled sheet of paper before it stopped.

5. We read *The Secret Garden* last year in my English class.

6. The alarm clock woke me at six this morning.

7. Call them before you leave for school.

8. The Nelsons ate dinner with the Gardeners.

APPLY **Add a direct object to each sentence below.**

9. The truck driver delivered _____ to our office.

10. Dr. Kumar told _____ that the procedure went well.

11. The squirrel hid _____ in the flowerpots on our porch.

12. Malik baked _____ for tomorrow's book club.

13. Before we can leave, you need to close _____.

14. I made _____ during art class today.

15. Hailey studied _____ at college last year.

Write a paragraph describing your morning routine. Circle the direct objects in your sentences.

_____

_____

_____

_____

_____

_____

Prefixes *con-* and *mid-*

FOCUS The prefix *con-* means "with" or "together." For example, when the prefix *con-* is added to the word *form,* the new word *conform* means "to form, or shape, with."

The prefix *mid-* means "middle." For example, the word *midweek* means "middle of the week."

PRACTICE Add *con-* or *mid-* to each base word below, and then write the new word's definition on the line. Use a dictionary if you need help.

1. _____year

_____

2. _____month

_____

3. _____struct

_____

4. _____centrate

_____

5. _____sequence

_____

6. _____night

_____

APPLY Each word below uses the prefix *con-* or *mid-*. Use your knowledge of the base word or root's meaning to write an original sentence for each word.

7. conference _____

_____

8. midwinter _____

_____

9. midmorning _____

_____

10. congregate _____

_____

11. midair _____

_____

12. convince _____

_____

13. midway _____

_____

14. conclude _____

_____

Vocabulary

FOCUS Review the selection vocabulary words from "Hatchet."

flue	registered
glancing	segment
painstaking	skittered
pointed	tendrils
quantity	tensed
rasping	wincing

PRACTICE Read each sentence. Think about the meaning of the underlined word or words. Write the vocabulary word on the line that is similar in meaning.

1. The cockroach <u>moved quickly</u> when the light shined on it.

_____

2. After the concert, he talked with a <u>rough, screeching</u> voice.

_____

3. It was a <u>careful and thorough</u> process to sort the tiny doll shoes.

_____

4. The man chopped the tree with <u>angled</u> hits to the trunk.

_____

5. The <u>amount</u> of toothpicks it takes to build a model bridge is great.

_____

6. The smoke went out through the <u>chimney</u> of the small hut.

_____

7. Make sure you use the <u>sharp</u> end of the stick.

_____

8. Matthew was <u>making a pained expression</u> when he twisted his ankle.

_____

9. We will read only a <u>part</u> of the story today in class.

_____

10. Every muscle in his body <u>tightened</u> when his sister scared him.

_____

11. <u>Thin, curly pieces</u> of ribbon decorated the wrapped gift.

_____

12. I finally <u>recognized</u> the buzzing sound as my alarm.

_____

APPLY Read each question. Think about the meaning of the underlined vocabulary word. Write your answers on the line.

13. What might cause a <u>rasping</u> voice?

_____

14. What is something that is <u>painstaking</u> to do?

_____

15. What is something you have seen that <u>skittered</u> as it moved?

_____

16. When would you have <u>tensed</u> your muscles?

_____

Practice Vocabulary • *Skills Practice 1*

Band Time

In music class, Mr. Everhart set out eight different instruments in their cases and said, "We will be starting Beginning Band next month. Today, I will give you a brief introduction to each instrument and you can decide which ones you might want to play. Talk to your parents about your favorites and then come back next Tuesday to try playing the ones you like before you decide."

Mr. Everhart explained that he had three types of instruments: brass, woodwinds, and percussion. He explained that in addition to the bass drum and snare drum, other instruments are also included in the percussion section: cymbals, shakers, chimes, and xylophones. He demonstrated the bass drum by hitting it with a glancing blow in a steady rhythm: boom…boom…boom…boom. Then he played the snare drum. It had a higher and crisper sound: rat-a-tat-tat, rat-a-tat-tat. I winced at the sound.

Mr. Everhart said, "You have three woodwind instruments you can choose: the flute, the clarinet, and the saxophone." He picked up a small case with a silver instrument in three segments. He fit the segments together, set his lip next to the hole, and blew across the hole. The flute made a sound that reminded me of an easy breeze. The next instrument was black and was stored in five segments! He put the segments together and played the low and mysterious sound of the clarinet. The notes were like smoke drifting and swirling around the room and out a chimney's flue.

In a big rectangular case, there was a bright yellow instrument with buttons that Mr. Everhart called keys. He told us that even though the saxophone looks like a brass instrument, it is a woodwind because of the mouthpiece. He pulled out the pointed mouthpiece and showed us the reed and then set the saxophone mouthpiece next to the clarinet mouthpiece, so we could see how they were alike. The saxophone had a brighter sound than the clarinet, but it was not for me.

"And now we have reached the brass instruments," said Mr. Everhart. "These instruments are played by making a buzzing sound into the mouthpiece." We all had to mimic Mr. Everhart's funny noise. He then played the trumpet, which was brighter still than the saxophone. The next instrument was the lower, mellower sound of the trombone. He saved the biggest and lowest sound for last.

"Most beginning players do not play tuba, but I do, and I thought you might like to hear it." He picked up the huge instrument, and I tensed awaiting to hear the massive sound. It wasn't as loud as I thought it would be. A low rumbling sound came out of the large bell that pointed to the ceiling.

"Our school has instruments that you may borrow, so your family will not need to purchase an instrument, however we have limited quantities. So, everyone may not get their first choice for an instrument. Talk over your options with your parents. You will need to practice some at home," finished Mr. Everhart with a rasping voice.

I went home that night and painstakingly shared every detail of all the instruments with my parents. I told them I was unsure which instrument I wanted to play. I liked the sounds of the clarinet and the trombone best, but they seemed very different. My parents said, "You can try them both out next Tuesday and we'll see which one you like best then."

I kept thinking about which one I liked better, so I talked to my friends. They said, "Girls play clarinet and boys play trombone." Well, that sounded like the silliest thing I ever heard. So, the more I asked people about my decision, the more I heard, "Girls can't play trombone." It bothered me when people said this, but I wasn't sure why. Then it registered what was bothering me: *No one tells me what I can and cannot do! I will show them that girls can play trombone!* I started buzzing my lips like Mr. Everhart showed us in class, just to prove everyone wrong.

When Tuesday arrived, I tried playing the clarinet, but it just squawked. It did not have the cool, dark sound that Mr. Everhart made. I was disappointed and hoped I would have much better luck with the trombone. I tucked a tendril of my hair behind my ear and picked up the trombone. I set the bell end on my shoulder and brought the mouthpiece up to my lips. I made the buzzing sound and this amazing mellow sound came out the other end!

"Bravo!" said Mr. Everhart. "I think you have found your voice in this band."

Cause and Effect

FOCUS
- A **cause** is the reason an event happens.
- An **effect** is what happens as a result of a cause.

The words *because, since, therefore,* and *so* show the reader that a cause-and-effect relationship has taken place.

PRACTICE Complete each cause-and-effect relationship below by providing the missing half.

1. My bike had a flat tire, so _____

_____

2. I forgot my lunch at home, so _____

_____

3. Because the ground was muddy, _____

_____

4. Eli loved Tuesdays because _____

_____

5. The library closes at six today; therefore, _____

_____

APPLY Read the sentences below, and identify the cause and effect in each one.

6. The leaves blew off the tree because the wind was so strong.

    Effect: _____

    Cause: _____

7. I could not reach the top shelf because I am too short.

    Effect: _____

    Cause: _____

8. We won the game, so we will play in the championship.

    Effect: _____

    Cause: _____

9. Because our family loves playing along the shore, we go to the beach often.

    Effect: _____

    Cause: _____

10. I did not study, so I did terribly on the test.

    Effect: _____

    Cause: _____

Access Complex Text • *Skills Practice 1*

Opinion Writing

Think

Audience: Who will read your opinion essay?

_____

Purpose: What is your reason for writing an opinion essay?

_____

PREWRITING On the lines below, list five possible sources for researching your topic.

Source # 1: _____

Source # 2: _____

Source # 3: _____

Source # 4: _____

Source # 5: _____

**Which is the best source for you to look in first?
Explain your answer.**

_____

_____

_____

_____

Revising

Use this checklist to revise your opinion essay.

☐ Does your writing have an effective introduction that clearly states an opinion?

☐ Does your writing have three reasons that support your opinion?

☐ Does each reason have a further explanation?

☐ Did you include at least one fact or reason taken from a source?

☐ Does your writing focus on a specific audience?

☐ Does your writing have an effective conclusion that sums up your opinion?

Editing/Proofreading

Use this checklist to correct mistakes in your opinion essay.

☐ Did you use proofreading symbols when editing?

☐ Did you include transition words and phrases to link ideas?

☐ Did you include prepositions and prepositional phrases where they are needed?

☐ Did you check your writing for spelling mistakes?

Publishing

Use this checklist to prepare your opinion writing for publishing.

☐ Write or type a neat copy of your opinion writing.

☐ Add a photograph or a drawing.

Name _____ **Date** _____

Prefixes *con-* and *mid-*

> ***FOCUS*** A prefix changes the meaning of the base or root word it precedes. Identifying prefixes and understanding their meanings can help you figure the meaning and spelling of difficult or unfamiliar word.
> - The suffix *con-* means "with" or "together."
> - The suffix *mid-* means "middle."

PRACTICE Add the prefix *con-* or *mid-* to the following base words and word parts, and write the resulting spelling words on the lines.

Word List
1. concoct
2. concur
3. conduct
4. conductor
5. confer
6. conjoin
7. conspire
8. construct
9. contract
10. converge
11. midair
12. midday
13. midnight
14. midpoint
15. midsentence
16. midstream
17. midterm
18. midtown
19. midway
20. midwinter

Challenge Words
1. contiguous
2. connote
3. midfielder

1. night _____
2. struct _____
3. cur _____
4. day _____
5. way _____
6. spire _____
7. stream _____
8. point _____
9. ductor _____
10. air _____
11. tract _____
12. fer _____
13. sentence _____
14. verge _____
15. term _____
16. coct _____

Skills Practice 1 • Spelling

UNIT 1 • Lesson 5 **67**

17. town _____   **19.** join _____

18. winter _____   **20.** duct _____

APPLY If the underlined word in the sentence is incorrect, write the correct word on the line. If it is correct, write *Correct.*

21. The two groups of hikers expect to <u>convurge</u> where
the trails meet.   _____

22. The boat traveled <u>midstreem</u> for most of the journey.   _____

23. I have stayed up until <u>midnite</u> only once.   _____

24. They will sign the <u>contrakt</u> at her office later today.   _____

25. We have our <u>miday</u> break at 11:30.   _____

26. The man in the tuxedo is the orchestra's <u>condoctor</u>.   _____

27. The bad guys in this movie will <u>cunspire</u> to rob the train. _____

28. My sister interrupted me <u>midsentence</u> with her loud laugh. _____

29. We all <u>concer</u> that Max had the best idea.   _____

30. Wednesday is the <u>midpoynt</u> of the week.   _____

31. The school hopes to <u>cunstuc</u> a new library and media center. _____

32. Our <u>midturm</u> reports are due on Friday.   _____

Prepositions and Prepositional Phrases

> **FOCUS**
> - A **preposition** relates a noun or pronoun to the rest of the sentence. They are used to show locations, time, and directions, or to provide additional details.
>   He visited the house **near** the river.
>   My glass **of** water spilled **across** the desk.
> - The noun or pronoun that follows the preposition is the **object of the preposition**.
>   The book *on the* **shelf** can be returned *to the* **library**.
> - A **prepositional phrase** is a group of words that begins with a preposition and ends with the object of the preposition.
>   We need to review adverbs **before the weekend**.
>   The new student **in our class** is the son **of a famous singer**.

PRACTICE Underline the prepositional phrase(s) in each of the following sentences.

1. Yao always took the same path to school.

2. Darren enjoyed visiting the animal shelter near our school.

3. Hannah loves playing with her puppy in the early morning.

4. After the game, Nitesh raced home to watch the news.

5. Before his exercise routine, Gary always makes sure to drink plenty of water.

6. During the storm, we stayed in the basement.

7. At work, Juan is always very courteous.

8. Gene walked across the street to his friend's house.

9. The colony in the New World grew slowly during its earliest years.

10. My father works for a large company downtown.

APPLY Create a prepositional phrase using the preposition in parentheses and use it in a sentence. Write the sentence on the lines.

11. (under) _____

_____

_____

12. (from) _____

_____

_____

13. (beside) _____

_____

_____

14. (against) _____

_____

_____

15. (above) _____

_____

_____

16. (after) _____

_____

_____

Wilderness Lessons

Alejandro looked at the camping gear spread on the floor. "I have to carry all this stuff on my back?" he asked.

"You bet," said Santiago. "This is a ten-day trek. I sent all the trip information pamphlets to you, right?" It was true. Santiago had mailed him a stack of information about this hike in the Colorado Rockies. "Let me guess. You didn't even read it, right?"

Alejandro shrugged and grinned. Santiago sighed, "Well, at least you got some good boots," he said.

Alejandro held up a foot, admired his new hiking boots, and said "Yes, these boots are going to take me places."

"Well you still have to hike there—with all that gear on your back," Santiago joked.

The next morning, Santiago and Alejandro gathered with the rest of the group at a trailhead high on a remote mountain road. Santiago was a group leader, along with a college student named Sonia, who had been making this trek for years.

"Short day today," said Sonia, shouldering her pack. "We'll hike seven miles and set up camp at Sweet Meadow." Alejandro headed up the trail feeling confident and excited. After all, he was an accomplished athlete; he played soccer and tennis. Things went fine for the first mile, but then the hikers came to a stretch of trail that ascended narrow switchbacks over a ridge. About halfway up, Alejandro was completely out of breath and leaned against a rock wall, panting.

Santiago stopped. "How's it going?" he asked.

"Whew! We haven't gone far. Why is it so hard to climb?" Alejandro asked, huffing.

"Elevation," said Santiago. "We are eight thousand feet above sea level, and the air gets thinner the higher you go. It was all in the information pamphlets...."

"Okay, okay, I guess I should have looked them over." Alejandro heaved himself upright again.

When Alejandro finally reached Sweet Meadow with some other struggling hikers, the group had set up camp.

"That first day is a real challenge," said Sonia. "You think you're in shape until you try hauling fifty pounds of gear at this elevation. It takes some getting used to."

"Oh, I am feeling fine," Alejandro claimed. He did not want to seem weak. The group ate a quick dinner and got ready for bed.

"Twelve miles tomorrow, everyone," said Santiago.

The next morning, Alejandro's legs were so stiff he could barely hobble out of the tent. He could not believe how much his knees and calves ached and throbbed. For the first time he doubted he had the tenacity to complete this trek.

Santiago saw his friend shuffle slowly to the campfire. "Don't worry too much, Alejandro. You'll feel better when we get going.

Miles one and two went by fairly well, but before he knew it, Alejandro was gasping in the thin air. He had to stop and rest three times in half an hour. Alejandro's spirits sank as he again recalled that no sport had ever challenged him like this did. What if he could not make it on this trip? The rest of the day did not get any easier—in fact, it was brutal. Every time Alejandro had to stop and rest, a voice in his head would tell him to quit, but then another voice would pipe in and make him keep moving. Finally, after twelve long miles, Alejandro limped into camp, heaved off his pack, and joined the group by the campfire.

"Way to go, Alejandro," said Sonia. "I'm impressed you're sticking with it."

Later, Santiago helped Alejandro dress the blisters on his feet for the next day. "Even great boots need to be broken in when they're new," he said.

The next day the group covered ten miles. Alejandro still felt sore and short of breath, but maybe not quite as much. He even glanced around the picturesque surroundings. "Wow, this really is extraordinary," he thought as he watched a herd of elk move through the valley below. Every day Alejandro felt a little better. He could hike faster, and he did not have to contemplate every step he was taking. On day six the group planned to scale Storm King, a fourteen-thousand-foot peak.

"Ready for this, Alejandro?" Santiago asked.

"I think so," said Alejandro. "I went through the checklist a few times, but ultimately I'm just going to pace myself."

"That's the only way to do it, friend," said Santiago. "You have to respect the wilderness. It's a place where you can learn some things about yourself."

"I definitely feel like I've been through some wilderness lessons," said Alejandro. "Now let's see what Storm King has to teach us."

A Very Proper Hero

Born in the mid-1800s, young Mary Kingsley was considered a very "proper" English girl. Throughout her childhood, she did what most girls like her did. Schools were only for boys, so she learned to read at home. When her mother fell sick, Kingsley stayed home and took care of her.

When she was thirty, both her parents died. She moved in with her brother to take care of his household. But one day her "proper" life changed completely. Kingsley's brother left for a long visit to China. She was free to do what she wanted. She headed straight for Africa.

As a girl, Kingsley had read dozens of books on natural history. She loved learning about plants and animals. And she longed to visit places English people knew little about. So in 1892 she set off for Africa.

Though raised in ease and comfort, Kingsley chose the rugged life. She traveled by steamship to the African coast and then went up rivers by steamboat and canoe. And she always traveled alone—a feat considered very daring for a woman of her time. To pay for the trip, she became a trader. She brought along pieces of cloth, which she exchanged for rubber. Rubber was rare in England, so she could sell it at a good price.

While in Africa, Kingsley met many of the local people and also other traders. Soon she knew much about life there. Africans became used to seeing this slender young woman in a prim black dress, never without her umbrella.

Kingsley enjoyed her time in Africa, but she did have some hair-raising adventures. One day, while walking through the jungle, she tumbled into a deep pit that was a trap set for animals. The bottom was lined with sharp spikes to stab the falling animal. Kingsley always wore several layers of skirts, as was the fashion in England. Luckily, the spikes could not get through them.

On another occasion, she was paddling a canoe along a stream when a hippo suddenly rose out of the water. Hippos do not like boats and can easily bite them in half. Kingsley could have attempted to flee, but she decided to make friends with the creature instead. As she wrote later, "I scratched him behind the ear with my umbrella, and we parted on good terms."

When Kingsley returned to London, she brought a little of Africa with her. A tiny pet monkey perched on her shoulder wherever she went.

In 1894 Kingsley made a second African trip. This time the British Museum hired her to bring back plants, animals, shells, and other things of interest. She collected hundreds of items. Three kinds of fish she found had never before been seen by Europeans. Scientists named the fish for her.

Nothing seemed to hold Kingsley back. One day she decided to climb Mount Cameroon, one of the highest volcanoes in Africa. She was the first European woman to do so. After reaching the top, she was caught in a tornado and nearly died. Not long after that, she came face-to-face with a gorilla. Few non-Africans had ever seen one before. In fact, many thought they were made-up creatures of legend. She also had some close calls with crocodiles, snakes, and other wild animals.

At the conclusion of this journey, Kingsley wrote a book titled *Travels in West Africa.* It was a huge best seller. She became a highly popular speaker as well. People flocked to her speeches to listen and to see Africa through a woman's eyes.

In 1899 Kingsley began a third trip. This time she went to South Africa. She had planned to collect more fish for the British Museum, but there was a war going on. England was fighting a group of settlers called the Boers for control of an area where gold had been found.

Kingsley immediately went to the army and offered to serve as a nurse in one of its hospitals. Instead, the army sent her to care for Boer soldiers in a prison camp. Conditions there were terrible. The air was full of deadly germs, and before long Kingsley caught typhoid fever. She died on June 3, 1900, at the age of thirty-seven.

In her short life, this "proper" young woman had accomplished things no other person—female or male—of her time could have done. An explorer, naturalist, humanitarian, author, and faithful daughter and sister, Kingsley was a hero many times over.

Name _____ **Date** _____

Vocabulary

FOCUS Review the selection vocabulary words from the next chapter of "Hatchet."

banked	interior
convulse	intervals
dormant	leathery
dusk	regulate
freshwater	swarmed
handle	weathered

PRACTICE Complete each sentence with a selection vocabulary word. Each vocabulary word should be used once.

1. We like to fish in the _____ lake outside of town.

2. The _____ covering of the chair was smooth to the touch.

3. Before starting the campfire for cooking, we _____ the wood in the center of the ring.

4. Just thinking about sucking on a lemon makes my body _____.

5. The _____ old fence needs to be painted this summer.

6. The outside of the house looked plain, but the _____ was beautiful.

7. These insects are _____ over the winter, and they become active in the spring.

8. The bats come out at _____ to eat the insects that come alive at night.

9. I do not know how I will _____ moving to a new school.

10. For exercise, I jump rope for _____ of two minutes.

11. It is easy to _____ the temperature with the new thermostat.

12. The fans _____ the players on the field after the big win.

APPLY Read each sentence. Use your knowledge of the vocabulary word's definition to answer each question.

13. You are eating outside at <u>dusk</u> with your family. What time of day is it?

_____

14. The grass is <u>dormant</u> over the winter. What does that mean?

_____

15. You are in the <u>interior</u> room of the museum. Where are you?

_____

16. You go through <u>intervals</u> of growing. What is happening?

_____

17. You <u>regulate</u> the noise level on the speaker. What are you doing?

_____

18. You can <u>handle</u> the responsibility of caring for a puppy. What does that mean?

_____

Practice Vocabulary • *Skills Practice 1*

A Summer Concert

Last summer, I saw my favorite singer at my first outdoor concert ever. I went with my family, and we arrived early to find our seats and get settled. At fifteen minute intervals, someone would come out and ask, "Are you ready?" to which we all responded, "Yeah!" and screamed. The concert was scheduled to start after dusk, so we still had an hour or so to wait.

This concert took place in a beautiful outdoor area, surrounded by tall trees that seemed to hug the weathered stage. In the distance, I watched the sun set over a large freshwater lake as the sky turned orange and pink and purple before night settled over us. The audience seemed calm, almost as if they were dormant, despite the underlying energy of expectation.

The people arrived little by little, filling in the seats, and soon almost every seat had a person waiting to see the great singer. Some people stood, while others sat looking around at the crowd and the scenery. I scoured the stage for signs of the singer, but I only found microphones, a drum set, a couple guitars, and two large screens to each side of the stage. Suddenly, the stage went completely dark.

I blinked my eyes and saw a bright light shining on the center of the stage while my favorite singer appeared in a black leather jacket, black pants, and a white T-shirt. He greeted the audience, asking, "How are you tonight?" Of course, we all answered with cheers and applause, which the band followed with a strong drum beat. The singer clapped his hands together, beating a regular interval with the band, urging us to do the same. Then, he started singing softly at first and gradually increasing the volume.

As the singer walked close to the front of the stage, fans were swarming around the edge and reaching out to him. I wondered how he would handle all those people crowding the stage as he sang. After running by with his hand outstretched, he would move to the back of the stage, and the crowd would settle back and pump their fists in the air to the music. Soon everyone at the concert swayed, danced, and convulsed to the beat of the music together, following the lead of the drummer and singing along with the music.

Before the last song, the singer reached into an interior pocket of his jacket and pulled out a folded letter. He addressed the audience, "Right here I have a special letter sent to me from a fan." The crowd cheered and clapped, whooped and hollered. He motioned for the crowd to quiet down, then continued, "and I want you to know how much the love and support of you all means to me. I keep this one close to my heart, and I read it before every performance. And, now I dedicate this next song to all my fans out there." The crowd went wild. I sang the last part with the whole crowd as loud as I could:

This song is for you, my tried and true! This song is for you, my tried and true!

We slowly made our way back to the car after the concert. I fell into the leathery interior of the car, not realizing how tired I was. I hummed the tunes to myself until I fell asleep, which did not take long.

We purchased the music from the concert to listen to at home. I think I sang those lines from the song all summer long. I am surprised my family did not regulate my musical selections after the concert. They had to be tired of hearing me repeat the same songs over and over, as I relived that warm, summer concert in my mind. I often wondered about the fan letter the singer mentioned. *What made the letter so memorable? Did the singer ever meet the person who wrote it? What did the letter say? How many letters does he read? Would he read a letter I wrote?*

In late summer, our family gathers around the fire pit in our backyard on Friday nights. My dad will bank the fire so it will last long into the night. Our neighbors often join us, and we gather around the fire to talk about our favorite memories. I shared my favorite memory of singing along with a whole crowd of people at the outdoor concert of my favorite singer. I could not imagine a better night, other than these nights when I can relive it with my family and friends.

Apply Vocabulary • *Skills Practice 1*

Main Idea and Details

FOCUS Authors organize their writing into a main idea supported by details.

- A main idea should be clear and focused.
- A main idea should have supporting details. Details provide additional information about the main idea.

PRACTICE Read the paragraph below. Identify the main idea of each paragraph and write it on the line. Then, write two details from the paragraph that support the main idea.

As a young boy, Jonah wanted to help the children he saw who looked hungry. So, he made them sandwiches and shared them with the children. Later, he saw they needed new socks and shoes. So, he asked people to donate new socks and shoes. In school, he noticed some children needed new book bags, so he asked people to help again. Soon his classmates had backpacks and supplies for school. He started a charity to keep the donations coming to help other children in his community. Helping others is a way of life for Jonah.

Main Idea:

1. _____

_____

Details:

2. _____

_____

3. _____

_____

APPLY Write a main idea sentence for each set of details.

4. The sun is shining. The birds are singing. The flowers are blooming. Children are outside playing.

_____

_____

5. You can read a book. You can play a game. You can write poetry. You can write a letter to a friend.

_____

_____

6. First, we saw the zebras in a large field exhibit. Next, we looked for the lions and tigers. Then, we found the large elephants. Finally, we saw a giraffe and her baby.

_____

_____

Write details for each main idea sentence.

7. This is going to be a busy week.

_____

_____

_____

8. The library is full of information.

_____

_____

_____

Access Complex Text • *Skills Practice 1*

Suffixes *-ant/-ent* and *-al/-ial*

FOCUS The suffix *-ant/-ent* means "one who" or "characterized by." The suffix *-ant/-ent* forms an adjective or noun. For example, the verb *serve* becomes a noun, *servant,* meaning "one who serves." The verb *excel* becomes an adjective, *excellent,* which means "characterized by excelling."

The suffix *-al/-ial* means "having characteristics of." The suffix *-al/-ial* usually forms an adjective or noun. For example, the noun *president* becomes an adjective, *presidential,* meaning "having characteristics of a president." The verb *refuse* becomes a noun, *refusal,* meaning "having characteristics of refusing."

PRACTICE **Complete each sentence below using the boldfaced word and the suffix *-ant/-ent*.**

1. Someone who **assists** is a(n) _____.

2. Something with the quality of **depending** is _____.

3. Someone who **occupies** a room is a(n) _____.

4. Something with the quality of **fluency** is _____.

Complete each sentence below using the boldface word and the suffix *-al/-ial*.

5. Something with the characteristics of **agriculture** is _____.

6. Something with the characteristics of **emotions** is _____.

7. Something with the characteristics of an **office** is _____.

8. Something with the characteristics of **industry** is _____.

APPLY Complete the "word-math" problems below by combining the base word and suffix and writing the word on the line. Then use each word in a sentence.

9. option + al = _____

_____

_____

10. depend + ent = _____

_____

_____

11. nation + al = _____

_____

_____

12. preside + ent = _____

_____

_____

13. substance + ial = _____

_____

_____

14. assist + ant = _____

_____

_____

Word Analysis • *Skills Practice 1*

Vocabulary

FOCUS Review the selection vocabulary words from "Monsoons: From Myth to Modern Science."

basins	proclamation
commanded	reliable
ebb	temperate
hydroelectric	tender
mature	turbines
prevailing	ushers

PRACTICE Complete each sentence with a selection vocabulary word. Each vocabulary word should be used once.

1. The king made a(n) _____ that there would be a day of celebration.

2. The _____ power plant provides electricity to the whole city.

3. Scientists are studying fish in river _____ around the United States.

4. I need a(n) _____ alarm clock if I am going to wake up on time every morning.

5. The general _____ the soldiers to march to the next town five miles away.

6. The _____ practice for recycling in our community is a weekly pick-up.

7. The big wind _____ turn slowly in the light breeze.

8. Because of the _____ climate, farmers have a long growing season.

9. I find it relaxing to watch the _____ and flow of the waves at the beach.

10. The rain _____ in some cool relief after the hot, sweltering days of summer.

11. The thin branches of the young trees are _____ and will break easily.

12. The _____ trees in the garden are tall and full of leaves, providing much shade.

APPLY Read each question. Write your answers and explanations in a complete sentence on the lines.

13. Which one is *mature*: a tadpole or a frog? Why? _____

_____

14. Which is a *reliable* spelling resource: a dictionary or a friend? Why? _____

_____

15. Which is *temperate*: Tennessee or northern Minnesota? Why? _____

_____

16. Which one is *tender*: a strained muscle or a relaxed muscle? Why? _____

_____

17. What is the *prevailing* transportation for school: a school bus or a truck? Why? _____

_____

18. Who can issue a *proclamation*: a principal or a student? Why? _____

_____

Name _____ Date _____

Power for All

Power to the People

In 1933, when Franklin D. Roosevelt was ushered into office by the American voters, the country was in a great depression. The prices of farm crops had fallen, making it hard for farmers and their families. One in four adults was looking for a job, on which families relied to have enough money for food and housing. He won the election on the prevailing opinion that the government needed to do something to help the millions of people out of work. He proclaimed that his "New Deal" would provide help in getting people jobs through a variety of government programs.

One of the programs during this time, the Tennessee Valley Authority (TVA), was created with the purpose of bringing electric power to the rural communities. To achieve this goal, the TVA planned to use the water from the river basins in the area to create hydroelectric power. The guiding commandment of the TVA was "Power to the People."

Today, almost everyone can get electricity to power their homes. As the technology for making electricity matures, new ways are created and improved upon to make it more affordable and available for all. Scientists now look to the sun, wind, and oceans for other ways to create electricity.

Solar Energy

What is solar energy? Solar energy refers to energy from the sun. The sun provides a great deal of energy to Earth as its rays hit Earth's surface. The problem is to figure out a way to collect this energy. Scientists are constantly trying to improve the ways we collect energy from the sun.

To do this, scientists have created solar panels which collect the sun's energy. These panels can be placed on roofs or on the ground, and then the energy is used to create electricity. Sometimes, power companies will give people a discount if they use solar panels to help power their homes. In temperate climates, where the sun shines most days, solar energy is becoming more common.

But what do you do if the sun does not shine almost every day?

Do you have nearby oceans or mountains or plains? Do you have wind in your community? Have you seen wind strong enough to bend tender, young trees? Scientists have been working on technology to create electricity from the wind.

Wind Power

Wind turbines look like large fans, which are moved by the power of the wind. The blades turn faster when the wind is stronger. As the blades turn, the turbine collects the energy of the wind that will then be used to make electricity. Wind farms are groups of wind turbines working together to make electricity.

People have been using windmills to run water pumps and provide electricity in rural communities for a long time. In fact, ancient Egypt used wind power to grind grain and pump water thousands of years ago. Wind turbines can be used in all fifty states, with both large and small turbines depending on the electricity needs in the area. Large turbines reach high into the sky, where there is more wind. They are used to create a great deal of electricity. Small turbines can be used to create electricity for a house or farm.

Offshore turbines are made to collect wind power in oceans, lakes, or other major water sources, where the wind is strong. Offshore turbines are even larger than the ones on land, and can collect this plentiful resource. The electricity is sent along cables under the sea to land. In addition to using wind from the oceans, scientists are also studying other ways to use energy in the ocean.

Ocean Power

Scientists are considering ways to use ocean tides, currents, or ocean waves to create electricity. However, there are many problems that need to be solved before this will work. Collecting that energy may create problems for ocean life and may interfere with migration patterns. Scientists are still researching and inventing ways to address the challenges of harnessing the power of the ocean.

If you sit on a beach watching the ebb and flow of the ocean waves, you can imagine all the power Earth provides. Feel the warm sun as you sit on the beach. Consider how those warm rays can be saved in solar batteries. Feel the gentle breeze as you look over the water. Imagine the blades of a wind turbine slowly turning and collecting energy. Wonder at the waves crashing on the beach as the tide goes in. Think about how that energy, too, might provide electricity to all.

Fact and Opinion

FOCUS Good writers use both facts and opinions in their writing. A good reader can tell one from the other.

- **Facts** are details that can be proven true or false.
- **Opinions** are what people think. They cannot be proven true or false.

PRACTICE Read each sentence below and tell whether it is a fact or an opinion.

1. The princess is the daughter of the king. _____

2. The princess is the kindest person in the kingdom. _____

3. Thúy Tinh returned after the princess married Són Tinh. _____

4. The king looked proudly at the happy couple. _____

5. The nation of Vietnam lies in Southeast Asia. _____

6. Vietnam is surrounded on three sides by China, Cambodia, and Laos. _____

7. The best time to visit Vietnam is in November. _____

8. Vietnam has two kinds of climates: temperate and tropical. _____

9. Too much rain is a bigger problem than not enough rain. _____

10. Water collected during the rainy season is used to produce hydroelectric power.

_____

APPLY Write one fact and one opinion you have about each topic below. Use complete sentences.

11. a local park

Fact: _____

Opinion: _____

12. games

Fact: _____

Opinion: _____

13. a book you read recently

Fact: _____

Opinion: _____

14. vegetables

Fact: _____

Opinion: _____

15. weather

Fact: _____

Opinion: _____

Access Complex Text • *Skills Practice 1*

Informational Writing

Think

Audience: Who will read your informational writing?

_____

Purpose: What is your reason for writing an informational text?

_____

PREWRITING Use the "note cards" below to take notes as you research. Be sure to use your own words as you take notes, and include details about the source where you found the information.

Notes: _____

_____

Source title: _____ **Source author:** _____

Page number: _____

Notes: _____

_____

Source title: _____ **Source author:** _____

Page number: _____

Revising When revising, be sure to look for places where you can eliminate irrelevant, or unnecessary, information. In informational writing, you also want to avoid including opinions that are not supported by facts. Read each paragraph below. Underline the sentences that contain irrelevant information or express an opinion.

Wind has been used as an energy source for thousands of years. Sailboats powered by the wind are an ancient form of transportation, and even the earliest windmills were in used in China nearly 4,000 years ago. The capitol of China is Beijing, and nearly twelve million people live there. Today, wind energy is used more and more around the world to generate electricity. In fact, nearly a quarter of the electricity used in Iowa and South Dakota was made with wind power. Wind power is the best way to create electricity.

Have you ever heard of a sport called *cricket?* Cricket is played with two teams of eleven players each. In some ways it is similar to baseball. Each team has batters that are trying to hit a ball and score points. The person who throws the ball is not called a pitcher, though. The bowler is the person who throws the ball. Bowling is a sport I like too. I try to go bowling at least once a month or so. The bowler throws the ball and tries to knock down a target that is right behind the batter. If the bowler hits the target, then the batter is out.

Suffixes *-ant/-ent* and *-al/-ial*

FOCUS
- The **suffixes** *-ant* and *-ent* both mean "one who" when added to words to form nouns. When added to words to form adjectives, the meaning of both suffixes is "characterized by."
- The suffix *-al/-ial* means "having characteristics of." It usually forms an adjective.

PRACTICE Add the suffix *-ant* or *-ent* to the following word parts to form spelling words on the lines.

Word List		Challenge Words
1. absorbent	11. obedient	1. celestial
2. aerial	12. occupant	2. centennial
3. artificial	13. partial	3. inhabitant
4. attendant	14. patient	
5. dependent	15. persistent	
6. essential	16. professional	
7. horizontal	17. radiant	
8. ignorant	18. renewal	
9. international	19. tolerant	
10. material	20. verbal	

1. pati _____

2. obedi _____

3. attend _____

4. toler _____

5. ignor _____

6. absorb _____

7. persist _____

8. depend _____

9. radi _____

10. occup _____

Add the suffix -al or -ial to the following word parts and write the resulting spelling words on the lines.

11. mater _____   _____

12. horizont _____   _____

13. profession _____ _____

14. verb _____   _____

15. artific _____   _____

16. essent _____   _____

17. renew _____   _____

18. aer _____   _____

19. internation _____ _____

20. part _____   _____

APPLY Circle the misspelled word in each sentence and write it correctly on the line.

21. The occupent was persistent about getting the leak fixed. _____

22. It is essental that the patient gets a lot of rest. _____

23. You need strong verbial skills to be a professional announcer. _____

24. This jacket was made using an absorbant material. _____

25. She was ignorent about international affairs. _____

26. The rancher was dependent on his sheep being obediant. _____

Capitalization

FOCUS

- Always capitalize proper nouns. Days, months, holidays, city and state names, and all parts of street names are proper nouns and are capitalized.

  Thomas Jefferson, Franklin stove, Wednesday

  May, Veterans Day, Portland, Maine, West Third Avenue

- Personal titles are capitalized when they are part of a name. Abbreviations that are parts of proper nouns are also capitalized.

  Aunt Shelly, Dr. Stubbs, President Ford, Harold M. Knox, Jr.

- Most words in book titles are capitalized, including the first word, the last word, and all other important words in a title. Minor words, such as *the, of, an, for,* are typically not capitalized unless they are the first or last word.

  The Wind in the Willows; Everything on a Waffle

- All of the letters in acronyms that refer to proper nouns are capitalized.

  NATO, CIA, USA

- The first word of a quotation is capitalized when the quotation is a complete sentence.

  Patrick Henry is remembered for saying, "Give me liberty, or give me death."

PRACTICE Circle the words that should begin with a capital letter, and rewrite the sentence correctly on the lines.

1. the fourth of july celebrates the signing of the declaration of independence.

_____

_____

2. our first president, general george washington, said, "it is better to offer no excuse than a bad one."

_____

_____

3. "paul Revere's ride" was written more than a century ago by Henry Wadsworth longfellow.

_____

_____

APPLY **Draw three lines under each letter that should have been capitalized. Draw a slash through each letter that should not have been capitalized.**

My brother, Brian, attends Thomas Jefferson high school. Each labor day, a fundraiser is held to raise money for care, which is a group that fights hunger around the World. Tables filled with donated items line the High School's hallways. Everything is for sale. The school's Principal kicked off the event by announcing, "let the sale begin!"

While the sale was happening inside, games and other activities were being held on the lawn near n. Prescott street. I bought a raffle ticket, and I won a copy of _a corner of the universe_ by Ann m. Martin. The Coach of the Soccer Team, Mr. Harris, sat in a dunking booth. My mom's brother, uncle Louis, sent the Coach splashing into the water. It was the funniest thing I've ever seen!

Hyphenated Compound Words; Suffixes *-ic/-ical*

FOCUS **Hyphenated compound words** are compound words joined with a hyphen. Hyphenated compound words are usually adjectives, adverbs, or nouns. The meaning of a hyphenated compound word can usually be determined using the meaning of the individual words. If you are unsure if the word is hyphenated, check a dictionary.

The suffix *-ic/-ical* means "relating to." Adding *-ic/-ical* to a base word or root forms adjectives and sometimes nouns. For example, *artistic* means "relating to artists" and *musical* means "relating to music."

PRACTICE **On the lines below, write a definition for the hyphenated compound word. Use a dictionary if you need help.**

1. time-consuming: _____

2. empty-handed: _____

3. well-being: _____

Add the suffix *-ic/-ical* to each word. Then write the new definition on the lines.

4. archaeology _____

_____

5. athlete _____

_____

6. allergy _____

_____

APPLY Choose a word from the box to complete each sentence. Each sentence will contain a hyphenated compound word or a word with the suffix *-ic/-ical.* Write the word on the line.

artistic	fantastic	get-together	gymnastics	identical
father-in-law	musical	organic	practical	part-time

7. Our family had a(n) _____ trip to the park this past weekend.

8. The teenager will look for a(n) _____ job this summer.

9. We bought some _____ apples and peaches at the farm stand.

10. The _____ twins wore the same outfits to school.

11. Our family had a(n) _____ over the holiday weekend.

12. We watched a(n) _____ show on TV that included a lot of singing and dancing.

13. The woman's _____ is going to watch the kids while she works on a project.

14. The teacher was impressed with the young child's _____ abilities.

15. There will be a(n) _____ class in the gym beginning next week.

16. Let's work on a(n) _____ solution to the problem.

Word Analysis • *Skills Practice 1*

Vocabulary

FOCUS Review the selection vocabulary words from "Making Waves."

axis	**kicks up**
clockwise	**lap**
conversely	**sediment**
fences	**sustain**
gyre	**teeming**
integral	**velocity**

PRACTICE Read each sentence. Write the vocabulary word on the line that best completes each sentence.

1. If the wind causes the dirt to fly around, this disturbance _____ the dirt.

2. When the waves hit the shoreline gently, you hear the waves _____.

3. If you build an enclosure to keep livestock in a field, it _____ the animals in the field.

4. The debris in the ocean is joining the spiral of ocean currents, so it is now part of the ocean _____.

5. If the carousel moves in a circular motion like a clock, the ride turns _____.

6. The globe is tilted on an imaginary center line around which it turns, just like the _____ of the Earth.

7. If the captain measures the speed of the ship, this measurement tells the ship's _____.

8. When a choir supports a note in a song, the singers will _____ the note.

9. If a playground is full of active children, it is _____ with children having fun.

10. If scientists take a water sample and let small pieces fall to the bottom, they are letting the _____ settle.

11. If your dad gives an option that is the opposite of a previous statement, he is _____ giving another option.

12. Understanding the rules of the game is important, so it is _____ that you know all the rules.

APPLY Read each question. Think about the meaning of the underlined vocabulary word. Write your answer on the line.

13. How would you turn your body if you moved it clockwise? _____

14. What is integral to learning new things? _____

15. What helps sustain students' learning? _____

16. Where might you find a place teeming with fish? _____

17. What is something that moves at a high velocity? _____

18. What kicks up noise at school? _____

Reading My Way to the Water Park

Before the end of the school year, I always sign up for the summer reading program at our school. Each child who completes ten hours of reading in the first month of summer gets free admission to our town's local water park. This reward is integrally related to how much I read early in the summer. Those free admissions go fast, so converse to my typical reading practice, I read a lot early in the summer.

I am so excited when I exchange my finished reading log for a free water park admission. The thought of having fun at the water park has sustained me through many hours of extra reading. Now I can make some plans with my family. The ticket comes with a map of the water park, and I immediately start planning my day. We set a date for next week, and I cannot wait!

The following week, as we walk up to the gates of the water park, I can see only a few rides that rise above the high walls that fence in the entire park. A large fountain with a slowly spinning globe appears in the front of the park. The globe is made of flowers and plants and slowly rotates on its axis. My family and I are in line to enter the park. As I wait, I look over the wall for the new ride, Geo Gyre.

Four people can ride together in a raft on the Geo Gyre. The ride starts up high, and you go around a set of spirals in a clockwise rotation, and then slide over the other side and go round and round counter-clockwise. The ride ends with a splash in a large pool. The shape and movement of the ride reminds me of the ocean gyres we learned about in school.

After waiting in line and putting on sunscreen, we get through the entrance gate. I cannot believe my eyes! It is teeming with families in bathing suits. I suppose I should have expected this, since it is a water park and a hot summer day, but the great quantity of people still surprises me. The Geo Gyre is to the right, and I notice there is an incredibly long line. So, I suggested that we go to the sandy-bottom pool first.

As I stand at the edge of the sandy-bottom pool, I listen to soft waves lapping at the sides of the pool. The water feels cool to my feet and legs, and I gradually go a little deeper into the water. However, this pool is not very deep, and the water only comes up to my knees. I feel the scratchy sand on my feet, and pick up some of the sediment with my toes. I drop the sand and watch it drift slowly down.

The wave pool is nearby, and soon we are in a much larger pool. There are no waves currently in the wave pool. It seems to me that waves are integral to a wave pool. Well, no sooner than I think this, I hear three loud beeps, and suddenly waves start kicking up. I am soon jumping and splashing in the waves with my family. Once the waves slow down, I suggest we go to the racing water slides.

The racing water slides are a series of four side–by–side water slides. One person goes down each slide, and each one goes at a different velocity, based on the slide. I pick the middle one, which looks like a very tall slide, but mostly straight. My family choose other slides that have more curves. It will be fun to see who will finish first. As we reach the bottom, our velocities are almost the same, but my dad gets to the end of the slide first!

We go back to the Geo Gyre, but the line still looks too long to wait. So, we decide to swim in the lazy river back to the wave pool. We will try again a little later. As we get back to the wave pool, a wind kicks up, and then a sudden rain shower. There is no thunder or lightning, but it is raining heavy rain drops. People grab their things and leave. We find a shelter, and wait.

I look up at the Geo Gyre and notice all the people are now gone. The rain and wind lessen, and soon we are walking up the stairs with a raft. We jump in the raft and travel round and round in the Geo Gyre. My heart is racing as we lean into the curves, ending with a big splash! It's the perfect end to the day!

Apply Vocabulary • *Skills Practice 1*

Classify and Categorize

FOCUS
- To **classify** is to identify the similarities that objects, characters, or events have in common with each other, and then grouping them by their similarities.
- To **categorize** is to organize the objects, characters, or events into groups, or categories.

PRACTICE On the diagram below, games are categorized into indoor and outdoor. Classify the games listed in the box by writing them in the appropriate category.

chess	jigsaw puzzle	basketball	tag
soccer	checkers	softball	bowling

1. **Indoor Games**

_____

_____

_____

2. **Outdoor Games**

_____

_____

_____

APPLY Classify the colors listed in the box by writing them under their appropriate categories.

| maroon | azure | gold | turquoise | crimson | cobalt |
| lemon | cherry | scarlet | amber | mustard | indigo |

3. Reds

_____

_____

_____

_____

4. Yellows

_____

_____

_____

_____

5. Blues

_____

_____

_____

_____

Access Complex Text • *Skills Practice 1*

Informational Writing

Citing Sources Citing the sources you use for research is an important part of avoiding plagiarism. A bibliography is a list of your sources that can be placed at the end of your writing. When you include a bibliography, you show readers that you have conducted research about your topic. Therefore, they can trust the information you have included, or they can look in the same sources to confirm what you have said. They can also use the bibliography if they want to look for more information about the topic.

Use the lines below to practice writing bibliographic entries for different types of sources. Fill in the information based on research you have already completed.

Citing a book: Author (Last Name, First Name). Title of book. City of publication: Publisher, Copyright date.

_____

_____

Citing an encyclopedia entry: Author (Last Name, First Name). "Title of entry." Title of encyclopedia. Edition or version. (If there is no author or main editor listed, just start with the title.)

_____

_____

Citing a web site: "Title of page or post." Title of Site. Year of post date or last update. Owner of site. Date accessed (month, day, year). <URL>. (URL is the full address of the web page)

_____

_____

Revising

Use this checklist to revise your informational writing.

☐ Does the writing clearly state the topic?

☐ Does the writing have an introduction that grabs the reader's attention?

☐ Does the writing include at least three important details about the topic?

☐ Are the details presented in the best, most logical order?

☐ Does the writing have any irrelevant information that can deleted?

☐ Does the writing have an effective conclusion that sums up the topic?

Editing/Proofreading

Use this checklist to correct mistakes in your informational writing.

☐ Did you use proofreading symbols when editing?

☐ Do all sentences end with the correct punctuation mark?

☐ Did you check the writing for misspelled words?

☐ Did you check the writing for mistakes in capitalization?

Publishing

Use this checklist to prepare your informational writing for publishing.

☐ Write or type a neat copy of your informational writing.

☐ Add a visual element that adds to the written information.

☐ Include a bibliography that cites sources used for research.

Hyphenated Compound Words and the Suffix *-ic/-ical*

FOCUS
- Compound words are words made up of two or more smaller words. Some compound words include hyphens between the smaller words. You must learn which compound words are **hyphenated compound words**.
- The **suffix *-ic/-ical*** means "relating to." It forms adjectives when added to base words.

PRACTICE Add the suffix *-ic* or *-ical* to the following base words or word parts and write the resulting spelling words on the line.

Word List
1. absent-minded
2. athletic
3. clinical
4. life-size
5. energetic
6. frantic
7. get-together
8. high-tech
9. historical
10. left-handed
11. long-distance
12. mythical
13. numerical
14. optimistic
15. patriotic
16. practical
17. self-respect
18. well-being
19. word-of-mouth
20. year-round

Challenge Words:
1. antiseptic
2. commander-in-chief
3. symmetrical

1. myth + ical = _____
2. frant + ic = _____
3. pract + ical = _____
4. number + ical = _____
5. history + ical = _____
6. clin + ical = _____
7. athlete + ic = _____
8. energy + ic = _____
9. optimism + ic = _____
10. patriot + ic = _____

Rewrite each compound word with the hyphens placed correctly.

11. longdistance _____

12. lifesize _____

13. hightech _____

14. selfrespect _____

15. yearround _____

16. wordofmouth _____

17. gettogether _____

18. wellbeing _____

19. absentminded _____

20. lefthanded _____

APPLY **If the spelling is incorrect, write the correct spelling on the line. Write *Correct* on the line if the spelling is correct.**

21. numberical _____

22. historical _____

23. get-to-gether _____

24. mithical _____

25. clinacal _____

26. patreotical _____

27. enurgetic _____

28. self-respect _____

29. year-around _____

30. anti-septical _____

Name _____ Date _____

Sentences and End Punctuation

FOCUS
- A **declarative** sentence makes a statement. It always ends with a period.

  My best friend is Reynaldo.

- An **interrogative** sentence asks a question. It ends with a question mark.

  Did you see the goal Ana scored?

- An **imperative** sentence gives a command or makes a request. It usually ends with a period.

  Please call the police.

- An **exclamatory** sentence expresses a strong feeling. It ends with an exclamation point.

  That was a yummy dessert!

- A **simple sentence** contains only one independent clause with a complete subject and a complete predicate. The subject of a simple sentence can be either simple or compound. The predicate can also be either simple or compound.

  The **students** visited a nature preserve. (simple subject)

  The students **visited a nature preserve**. (simple predicate)

  The **students** and their **teacher** visited a nature preserve. (compound subject)

  The students **visited a nature preserve** and **had a picnic**. (compound predicate)

PRACTICE Add the correct end punctuation to these sentences. Then write S on the lines of the simple sentences.

1. _____ Do you know anything about Alaska

2. _____ The United States bought Alaska from Russia in 1867

3. _____ Henry Seward was the Secretary of State at that time, and he arranged to purchase Alaska for $7 million

Skills Practice 1 • Grammar   UNIT 2 • Lesson 2 **107**

4. _____ People called the territory "Seward's Folly" because they thought it cost too much money

5. _____ You won't believe what happens next

6. _____ The discovery of gold started a rush to Alaska

7. _____ Tell me your favorite part of the story

APPLY Label the following sentences as declarative, interrogative, imperative, or exclamatory.

8. Where is Julio taking those boxes? _____

9. Stay with Trevor until I get back from the store. _____

10. While Mr. James jogged, his wife read at the library. _____

11. That is a very loud noise! _____

12. Listen as I tell you about my childhood. _____

13. You should eat five servings of produce each day. _____

14. Does Emily know when the next train is scheduled to arrive? _____

Write a simple sentence to meet each description in parentheses.

15. (with a compound subject) _____

_____

16. (with a simple predicate) _____

_____

Latin Root *terra*; Greek Roots *geo, photo*

> **FOCUS** Identifying and understanding Greek and Latin roots can help you define difficult and unfamiliar words. When you know the meaning of a root, you can determine the meanings of many words that contain that root.
>
> The Latin root *terra* means "land" or "Earth." For example, the word *terrain* means "a type of land." The Greek root *geo* means "Earth." For example, the word *geography* means "study of Earth's surface." The Greek root *photo* means "light." For example, the word *photograph* means "a picture created with the use of light."

PRACTICE **Read each word. Circle the roots *terra* (or *terr*), *geo*, or *photo* in each one. Then write the definition of the word on the line.**

1. terrain

_____

2. geographer

_____

3. photographer

_____

4. photocopier

_____

5. terra-cotta

_____

6. terrier

_____

APPLY Select the word with a Greek or Latin root that best fits the definition and write it on the line. Then use each word in a sentence.

geocentric	geode	geology	photocopy
photogenic	photosynthesis	territorial	territory

7. An area of land _____

_____

_____

8. A hollow rock that has crystals inside _____

_____

_____

9. Producing light; describes people who are photographed well _____

_____

_____

10. Study of rocks _____

_____

_____

11. A natural process in which light helps to create food for plants _____

_____

_____

12. To make a copy _____

_____

_____

13. Relating to the center of Earth _____

_____

_____

14. Having characteristics of land _____

_____

_____

Word Analysis • *Skills Practice 1*

Vocabulary

FOCUS Review the selection vocabulary words from "Ookpik" and "Critters Crossing!"

aerial	indifferent
ancestry	lurched
blustery	scurrying
downy	seldom
emerging	specialized
exceptionally	veered
functions	vegetation

PRACTICE Read each sentence. Think about the meaning of the underlined word or words. Write the vocabulary word on the line that is similar in meaning.

1. The driver <u>changed direction</u> to the right suddenly to avoid hitting a pothole.

   _____

2. The baby chick's <u>fuzzy, soft</u> feathers kept its body warm. _____

3. The student was <u>not often</u> late for school. _____

4. The photograph is from an interesting <u>above-ground</u> viewpoint. _____

5. The girl wore a thick coat on the <u>violently windy</u> day. _____

6. The truck <u>moved forward suddenly</u> and then broke down. _____

7. The main character was <u>rising to prominence</u> as the hero. _____

8. He was <u>not interested</u> about the outcome of the basketball game. _____

9. She was researching the <u>family history</u> of the town's settlers. _____

10. The parade was <u>unusually and unexpectedly</u> long this year. _____

11. The <u>plant life</u> is starting to bloom now that it is spring. _____

12. The mice were <u>moving quickly with small steps</u> on the floor. _____

13. The carpenter has <u>specifically-purposed</u> tools to ensure quality. _____

14. The <u>necessary actions</u> of an alarm clock are to tell time and to wake a sleeping person. _____

APPLY Read each question. Think about the meaning of the underlined vocabulary word. Write your answers on the line.

15. How might you take an <u>aerial</u> photograph?

_____

16. What is something you <u>seldom</u> do?

_____

17. When have you been <u>indifferent</u> about something?

_____

18. What is the <u>vegetation</u> like around your school?

_____

Finding the Perfect Gift

On a blustery January morning, Maria walked with her grandmother along the main street of their small downtown area. People scurried from store to store, trying to stay warm. Maria was grateful for her warm, down coat and pulled it closer to her body. Her grandmother veered into one of the shops, and Maria followed her, wondering what she might find inside.

Inside, Maria could tell that most of the items in the store were old. This must be the antique market that her grandmother described to her over the phone. Maria seldom went in the shops of the downtown area, but her grandmother liked to talk to all the owners and see what each sold. They were looking for a gift to give her grandfather. Maria held up an old watch and asked, "What about this?"

Grandmother responded, "Is it functional? Although your grandfather likes to put things together, he would need help making it work!" Maria asked the sales clerk if the watch functioned properly. It did not, so she placed it back where she found it. They continued to look around the shop at different items.

Maria noticed a little motorized truck and turned it on. It lurched around and then stopped. She turned it on and off again, and it did the same thing. She wanted to find a different kind of gift, but one that her grandfather would enjoy. Maria's grandmother found an old advertising poster. Maria looked at it indifferently, and then shook her head. She wanted something exceptional, not ordinary.

Maria and her grandmother continued to go through the market looking at many old things, including glassware, old tools, old furniture, and old artwork. They enjoyed discussing the possible uses of some of the items, imagining how their ancestors would have used some of the unidentifiable tools. Then, that prompted a discussion of her grandfather's ancestry.

They began looking for items that reflected his love of food, especially those foods that specialized in traditional methods. He loved breads made from hand-ground flour and butter made from old churns. So, then Maria and her grandmother began to look for old grinders or churns, but the shop did not have any of either of those items. Disappointed, Maria said, "As much as I hate to say it, we may need to brave the cold and check out another shop."

Maria and her grandmother bundled up and hurried to the shop next door. This store had specialty breads and cheeses. All the foods looked amazing. The shop also had a variety of meats and canned jams and jellies. They sampled some of the specialized cheeses made from local dairy. Maria's grandfather was a farmer who appreciated local foods. Her grandmother said he had enough at home.

As they were getting ready to leave, Maria looked out the large window and noticed a shop window across the street full of green vegetation. She exclaimed, "Look at all the plants in the shop across the street! Perhaps we will find something in that shop." Her grandmother agreed, and soon they were facing the blustery winds on their way to the shops across the street.

Inside the shop with the lush vegetation, Maria and her grandmother found many arrangements of plants and flowers. It was such a nice contrast to the weather outside, and they tried to imagine which one grandfather might enjoy. He liked to care for the plants outside of the house, but as grandmother reminded Maria, "Although he waters the outdoor plants in the summer, he seldom waters the plants inside the house. So, maybe we should check out another shop."

"I would love to find a shop that would make something one-of-a-kind," said Maria.

The shop owner suggested, "There is an exceptional emerging artist who has recently opened a shop just two doors down. Perhaps she could help you find that one-of-a-kind gift."

"That's a great idea, depending on the artwork she does," said Maria. "Well, what do you think?"

"I think we are running out of shops to find something, so let's go!" replied her grandmother.

Once again, they braved the blustery weather and scurried two doors down. They entered the shop, full of artwork. The artwork aerially illustrated local landscapes and vegetation from high above. It was interesting, but Maria was unsure. Then, she looked closer at the images in one of the pieces. She pointed to it and exclaimed, "This is it! This is the perfect gift!"

Maria and her grandmother looked more carefully at the artwork. They knew this place well, even if not from the aerial viewpoint. It was the farm where they lived, showing all that grandfather loved.

Apply Vocabulary • *Skills Practice 1*

Sequence

> **FOCUS** The **sequence** in which events occur in a story is indicated by time words and order words.

PRACTICE Read each sentence. Write the time and order word or phrase in each sentence on the line.

1. The children played kickball all summer in the backyard.

   _____

2. First, sign up for the reading program at your local library.

   _____

3. Next, read lots of books and record the books and time you read.

   _____

4. Then, turn in your completed list of books to the library.

   _____

5. You will receive a wonderful reading reward at last.

   _____

6. My brother started kindergarten this past fall.

   _____

7. Will you meet me after school to go to the library?

   _____

8. I finally found the book I wanted to read.

   _____

APPLY Read each paragraph below. Then, rewrite the events in the paragraph in the correct sequence.

9. I love to write stories, especially fairy tales. Next, I start drafting to tell the story. At long last, I am ready to share my story with others. Then, I go back and reread my draft, making notes to revise. First, I think up the characters and the problem. After I revise and edit my story, I draw some pictures to illustrate it. Once my draft is complete, I set it aside.

_____

_____

_____

_____

10. On Fridays, we watch a movie. My family does different activities each night of the week. On Tuesdays, we go to a park. On Thursdays, we play a game. On Mondays, we go to the library. Finally, over the weekends, we visit family. On Wednesdays, we listen to music together.

_____

_____

_____

_____

Informational Writing

Think

Audience: Who will read your informational writing?

_____

Purpose: What is your reason for writing?

_____

PREWRITING   Write the Science Category you have chosen in the center space. Generate Topic Ideas related to the category, and write them in the surrounding areas.

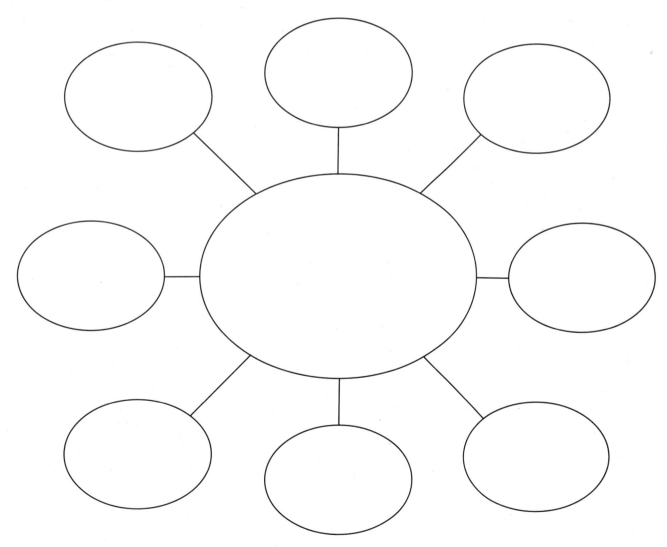

PREWRITING Use the lines below to make sure you have enough information for three paragraphs. Write the main detail that will be the topic for the paragraph. Then list additional facts, examples, or explanations related to the main detail.

Paragraph 1 Important Detail: _____

Related details: _____

_____

_____

_____

Paragraph 2 Important Detail: _____

Related details: _____

_____

_____

_____

Paragraph 3 Important Detail: _____

Related details: _____

_____

_____

_____

Writing • *Skills Practice 1*

Latin Root *terra* and Greek Roots *geo* and *photo*

FOCUS • Understanding and identifying Greek and Latin roots and their meanings can help you spell many new words. Here are some roots in the spelling words and their meanings:

Latin root *terra* = "land" or "Earth"; **Greek root *geo*** = "Earth"; **Greek root *photo*** = "light"

PRACTICE Fill in the root and write the resulting spelling word on the line. Use each spelling word only once.

Word List

1. geode
2. geography
3. geological
4. geologist
5. geometry
6. geothermal
7. Mediterranean
8. photocopy
9. photogenic
10. photographer
11. photographic
12. photography
13. photosynthesis
14. telephoto
15. terrace
16. terrain
17. terrarium
18. terrier
19. territorial
20. territory

Challenge Words:

1. extraterrestrial
2. photon
3. subterranean

1. _____ + ier = _____

2. _____ + grapher = _____

3. _____ + thermal = _____

4. Medi + _____ + anean = _____

5. _____ + itorial = _____

6. _____ + graphy = _____

7. _____ + logist = _____

8. _____ + genic = _____

9. _____ + itory = _____

10. _____ + de = _____

11. _____ + graphic = _____

12. _____ + graphy = _____

13. _____ + ain = _____

14. _____ + metry = _____

15. _____ + copy = _____

16. _____ + arium = _____

17. _____ + logical = _____

18. _____ + ace = _____

19. _____ + synthesis = _____

20. tele + _____ = _____

APPLY Write the spelling word that is represented by the following root meaning combinations.

21. "outside" + "Earth" = _____

22. "below" + "Earth" = _____

23. "light" + "writer" = _____

24. "distance" + "light" = _____

25. "Earth" + "heat" = _____

Choose the word that does not share the same main root as the other two and write it on the line.

26. geography, photogenic, geological _____

27. telephoto, territory, extraterrestrial _____

28. terrier, Mediterranean, photocopy _____

29. geography, geode, photon _____

30. geometry, territorial, territory _____

31. subterranean, geological, terrier _____

32. telephoto, terrier, photographer _____

Spelling • *Skills Practice 1*

Conjunctions

FOCUS A **conjunction** is a word that connects words or groups of words.

- A **coordinating conjunction** joins words or groups of words that are equally important in a sentence. The coordinating conjunctions are *and, but,* and *or.*

  My older brother **and** sister live in Atlanta.

  Lily will need to babysit tomorrow, **or** we cannot go to the movie.

- **Correlative conjunctions** work in pairs to join words and groups of words. The correlative conjunctions are *either/or* and *neither/nor.*

  Neither the birds **nor** the squirrels can get into the shed now.

- A **subordinating conjunction** joins two clauses when one clause is dependent on the other. Examples of subordinating conjunctions are *before, if, after, so, when,* and *because.*

  After Aunt Gina gets here, we will put out the food.

PRACTICE **Circle the conjunction(s) in each sentence. Then write C on the line if it is a coordinating or correlative conjunction. Write S on the line if it is a subordinating conjunction.**

1. We all ran inside before the rain poured down. _____

2. Aaron likes to go biking and jogging on the weekends. _____

3. The train left the station on time, but it arrived at the next stop two hours late. _____

4. Paul wanted to purchase either a baseball or a softball. _____

5. We returned the radio to the store because the speakers do not work. _____

6. Mr. Louis or Ms. Unser will find the book for you. _____

7. How will Olivia get here if the car is in the shop? _____

8. When you see the library on the corner, turn left. _____

APPLY Use coordinating and subordinating conjunctions to complete each sentence below.

9. The Suarezes planned to take Nitesh's boat and go sailing, _____ there was hardly any wind.

10. You need to decide whether we will have pizza, _____ you will make your famous meatloaf.

11. Dana's soccer team will either score on this kick, _____ the game will be over.

12. A door slammed somewhere in the house, _____ I heard my sister yelling.

13. Mountain climbing is a thrilling activity, _____ you need professional training before you can use Tim's gear.

14. Dante washed his face, brushed his teeth, _____ combed his hair before leaving the house.

15. _____ the game we will try to go to the store.

16. We hope to take our vacation in September _____ the weather gets too cold.

17. _____ the neighbors were being loud, Jimmy tried to go to sleep anyway.

18. Kathy had always wanted to go to a concert, _____ she finally got her chance.

19. _____ the sun sets, we cannot start the fireworks display.

20. I have not seen any deer in our yard _____ my dog, Chipper, chased them away.

Suffixes *-ity* and *-tion/-ation/-ition*

FOCUS The suffix *-ity* means "state of" or "quality of." The suffix *-ity* changes adjectives to nouns. For example, the adjective *active* becomes a noun, *activity,* meaning "quality of being active."

The suffix *-tion/-ation/-ition* means "act" or "process." The suffix *-tion/-ation/-ition* also forms nouns. For example, the verb *examine* becomes a noun, *examination,* meaning "act of examining."

PRACTICE Write the word from the box that matches each definition below.

definition	imagination	imposition
production	repetition	security

1. act of defining _____

2. state of being secure _____

3. act of imagining _____

4. act of producing _____

5. act of imposing _____

6. act of repeating _____

APPLY Each word below uses the suffix *-ity* or *-tion/-ation/-ition.* Use your knowledge of the base word or root's meaning to write an original sentence for each word.

7. convention _____

_____

8. priority _____

_____

9. admiration _____

_____

10. individuality _____

_____

11. agility _____

_____

12. nutrition _____

_____

13. reality _____

_____

14. competition _____

_____

Word Analysis • *Skills Practice 1*

Vocabulary

FOCUS Review the selection vocabulary words from "Salmon Creek."

camouflage	radiant
enclosing	sheen
estuary	smolt
lazed	swelling
lingered	tattered
quickening	torrent

PRACTICE Read each question. Choose the vocabulary word that answers the question and write it on the line.

1. If you see a young salmon, is it a <u>smolt</u> or a <u>sheen</u>?

_____

2. If you are rested all day last Saturday, does that mean you <u>lazed</u> or <u>lingered</u> all day?

_____

3. If a piece of clothing is torn and ragged, is it <u>radiant</u> or <u>tattered</u>?

_____

4. If a fence is surrounding a field on all sides, is it <u>enclosing</u> or <u>quickening</u> the field?

_____

5. If a hunter is disguised to blend into the surroundings, is the hunter trying to <u>camouflage</u> or <u>sheen</u> himself?

_____

6. If a stream is moving fast with a lot of water, is it a <u>torrent</u> or an <u>estuary</u>?

_____

7. If you find yourself at the mouth of a river, is it an <u>estuary</u> or a <u>sheen</u>?

_____

8. If a balloon is growing in size as you blow air into it, is it <u>swelling</u> or <u>quickening</u>?

_____

9. If someone is wearing a shiny top that reflects light, does it have a <u>sheen</u> or a <u>torrent?</u>

_____

10. If an animal is sleeping and then wakes and is becoming animated, is it <u>quickening</u> or <u>enclosing?</u>

_____

11. If you remained in the kitchen after dinner, have you <u>lingered</u> or <u>tattered</u> in the kitchen?

_____

12. If you notice the rich beautiful colors of a sunset, would you describe it as <u>camouflage</u> or <u>radiant?</u>

_____

APPLY Read each sentence. Answer each question by explaining the definition in your own words.

13. Your brother <u>lingered</u> in the new book section of the library. What is he doing?

_____

14. You polished the table until it had a nice <u>sheen</u>. What does that mean?

_____

15. The old towel was <u>tattered</u>, so you ripped it into rags. How did the old towel look?

_____

16. A friend twisted his ankle and it began <u>swelling</u>. What does that mean?

_____

17. The color of the grasshopper helps it <u>camouflage</u> itself in the grass. What did it do?

_____

18. The tree branches moved quickly in the <u>torrent</u> after the storm. What might it look like?

_____

Practice Vocabulary • *Skills Practice 1*

Camping

My family likes to go camping, so we spend quite a few weekends at the campground. Although I always complain about going camping, I find that I do enjoy lazing and reading in the hammock during the day. I love how we all linger around the fire at night and tell stories. I like it when I am snuggled into my sleeping bag, enclosed in the warmth like a cocoon. So, maybe it is not all bad.

Sometimes it rains overnight. If the rain is light, it makes a quiet tapping sound on the canvas tent top. If there is a torrential rain, water can seep into the tent, and even the bottom of the tent can get wet. On those nights, my family encloses the tent with an extra waterproof layer of material. As long as I have my tattered teddy bear, I feel like I can sleep almost anywhere.

When I am camping, I often wake to a light radiantly glowing through the trees or over a nearby lake. The warm colors gently push the darkness away, and suddenly I am wide awake. I hear the quiet chirps of the birds become louder as the day gets brighter. Then, I hear them quickening in the trees as they move from tree to tree singing. The sheen of the dew on the grass slowly fades as the day warms.

Although I am awake, I linger in my sleeping bag until I know the others are awake. We work together to make breakfast and clean up. We often use a sponge to clean up, and I love to watch it swell as I add water to it. Once the campsite is clean, we have time to play games, read, or explore. We often mix up the activities, however, my favorite thing to do is lazing in a shady spot with a book.

When I am not lazing in the hammock, I explore around the campsite with my brother and sister. We look for camouflaged insects and animals. One time, I found a walking stick on a tree—it took my sister forever to find it, even when I pointed directly at it. That is how well it camouflages itself with the branches on the tree! My brother always manages to find a frog or toad camouflaged in the grass or in a tree.

On our most recent camping trip, there was a small stream near our campsite. As we were exploring, my sister saw a bright sheen in the water. We could not tell at first if the light reflected off the water or off something in the water. Then, we saw these little fish.

We asked our parents if they knew what kind of fish they were. My father thought they might be smolt. I had never heard of smolt, and he told me about salmon and how they begin their lives in freshwater streams. He explained that they will grow and get bigger and then travel to the estuary where the stream meets the ocean. They will live in the ocean, and then return to this stream one day.

I asked if we could follow the journey that the little fish would take. I was curious to see the estuary where these little fish would one day go. He said we would not be able to walk it in one day, but we could take a little drive to the estuary for the day. We packed a lunch and jumped in the car.

I looked at the stream next to the road as we traveled by car. It was flowing in torrents from recent rains, and I imagined how big the smolt would need to grow to make this journey. We took a bridge over the stream and soon we arrived at the estuary. The stream now looked more like a river with a wide opening to the sea. We found a place to park and have our lunch, overlooking the water.

After lunch, we lingered around the estuary, exploring the new area. Like we did at the campsite, we looked for insects and animals that might be camouflaged in a tree or near the grass. We did not have much luck, but it was fun to look. Then, we set up some hammocks in the park overlooking the estuary, and lazed about reading or sleeping in the shade. When the radiant sun started to sit low in the sky, we decided to pack up and head back to the campsite.

Once we arrived back at our campsite, we fell into our regular routine. We had our dinner and told stories around the fire. It wasn't long before I snuggled up with my tattered teddy bear!

Apply Vocabulary • *Skills Practice 1*

Compare and Contrast

FOCUS
- When writers **compare,** they tell how things, ideas, events, or characters are alike.
- When writers **contrast,** they tell how things, ideas, events, or characters are different.

PRACTICE Read each sentence below. Decide if the sentence is showing a comparison or a contrast. Then, rewrite each sentence reflecting the other term.

1. My grandfather likes to fish, but my father prefers to golf.

   _____

2. My sister likes to play the flute, but I like to play the tuba.

   _____

3. A moth has wings and can fly, but an ant can only move on the ground.

   _____

4. Zack and Zoe are both learning to play hockey.

   _____

5. Both my brother and I like to go to the park to play.

   _____

6. The students and the teacher like to read poetry.

   _____

7. Daniella has a blue backpack, but Jenna has a red backpack.

   _____

8. Both Joe and Jordan walk to school every day.

   _____

APPLY On the lines below, compare and contrast two things each about sunrise and sunset.

9. **Compare:** _____

_____

_____

_____

_____

10. **Contrast:** _____

_____

_____

_____

_____

Access Complex Text • *Skills Practice 1*

Informational Writing

Revising

Transition words link ideas, sentences, and paragraphs to each other. Transition words make writing clearer and more accurate, and they help the reader move smoothly from one idea to another. They can show time (*today, this morning*), order (*first, next*), contrast (*however, on the other hand*), comparisons (*also, similarly*), additional information (*for example, in addition*), and conclusions (*finally, in summary*).

Circle the transition words in the paragraph below.

Both Tiana and Maya like swimming. However, Maya likes to swim freestyle, and Tiana prefers the butterfly stroke. Yesterday they practiced both strokes, and additionally they each swam the backstroke. This morning, both girls competed in a swim meet. As a result of her hard work, Tiana placed second in her race. Similarly, Maya took second place in her race.

Write sentences according to the descriptions.

1. Use a transition word that shows a comparison to describe two different pets.

   _____

   _____

   _____

2. Use a transition word that signals additional information to describe a school policy.

   _____

   _____

   _____

Revising

Use this checklist to revise your informational writing.

☐ Does the writing clearly state the topic?

☐ Does the writing have an introduction that grabs the reader's attention?

☐ Does the writing include at least three important details about the topic?

☐ Does the writing stay on topic?

☐ Does the writing repeat any words or phrases too often?

☐ Does the writing have an engaging conclusion that sums up the topic?

Editing/Proofreading

Use this checklist to correct mistakes in your informational writing.

☐ Did you use proofreading symbols when editing?

☐ Have you included transition words where they are needed?

☐ Have conjunctions been used correctly?

☐ Do all sentences end with the correct punctuation mark?

☐ Did you check the writing for misspelled words?

Publishing

Use this checklist to prepare your informational writing for publishing.

☐ Write or type a neat copy of your informational writing.

☐ Include a bibliography that cites sources used for research.

Suffixes *-ity* and *-tion/-ation/-ition*

FOCUS
- The **suffix *-ity*** means "state or quality of." When it is added to a base word, it forms a noun.
- The **suffix *-tion/-ation/-ition*** means "act or process." When it is added to a base word, it forms a noun.

PRACTICE On the lines, write the spelling words that are formed from the following base words and suffixes.

Word List

1. abbreviation
2. ambition
3. audition
4. composition
5. constellation
6. disability
7. exception
8. expedition
9. humanity
10. ignition
11. inspection
12. intention
13. population
14. possibility
15. precipitation
16. regulation
17. resolution
18. similarity
19. sincerity
20. subscription

Challenge Words

1. crystallization
2. malnutrition
3. practicality

1. intent + tion = _____

2. resolute + tion = _____

3. audit + ition = _____

4. subscribe + tion = _____

5. similar + ity = _____

6. ambi + tion = _____

7. human + ity = _____

8. expedite + ition = _____

9. precipitate + ation = _____

10. abbreviate + ation = _____

11. compose + ition = _____

12. disable + ity = _____

13. ignite + ition = _____

14. possible + ity = _____

15. except + tion = _____   **18.** constell + ation = _____

16. regulate + ation = _____   **19.** sincere + ity = _____

17. inspect + tion = _____   **20.** populate + ation = _____

APPLY On the line, write the spelling word that is related by a common root or base word to each of the following words.

21. impossible _____

22. able _____

23. receptacle _____

24. dissimilar _____

25. insincere _____

26. decompose _____

27. nutritious _____

28. impractical _____

29. respect _____

30. popular _____

31. reignite _____

32. pedestrian _____

33. deregulate _____

34. applaud _____

Compound Sentences

FOCUS A **compound sentence** consists of two or more simple sentences connected by a comma and a coordinating conjunction. The coordinating conjunctions are *and, but,* and *or.*

The band arrived at the concert hall**, but** the doors were still locked.

At the museum, we saw a model of downtown, **and** we designed a new building.

John was almost home, **but** then he got a flat tire.

PRACTICE **Combine each pair of sentences below into a single complete compound sentence. Write it on the lines.**

1. Dave wants to see a movie. I want to go skateboarding.

_____

_____

2. Shane met Donetta at the library. They studied together.

_____

_____

3. We can make dinner. We can order gyros.

_____

_____

4. Krista trimmed the bushes. Krista raked the leaves.

_____

_____

APPLY Place a checkmark next to each sentence that is a complete compound sentence and an X next to each compete simple sentence. Add the missing commas to the compound sentences.

5. _____ My friend and I built a model airplane and we displayed it at school.

6. _____ Our teacher was impressed with our finished product.

7. _____ Mr. Jefferson had flown the same kind of plane in the Air Force and he told us about his experiences.

8. _____ Paul always knew he would become a teacher or a pilot for an airline.

9. _____ He loves sharing his knowledge with others.

10. _____ We loved winter but we hated the inclement weather.

11. _____ The ending of the season was sad.

12. _____ We hiked all day to the top of the mountain and the view was spectacular.

Write two compound sentences about yourself, your school, or your neighborhood.

13. _____

_____

_____

14. _____

_____

_____

Latin Roots *sens, spec,* and *sim*

> **FOCUS** Latin roots are common in the English language. Identifying and understanding roots can help you define difficult and unfamiliar words. When you know the meaning of a root, you can determine the meanings of many words that contain that root.
>
> The Latin root *sens* means "be aware." For example, the word *sensor* means "something that senses or is aware." The Latin root *spec* means "see." For example, the word *inspect* means "to look at carefully." The Latin root *sim* means "like." For example, the word *similar* means "alike."

PRACTICE Think of a word that uses each Greek or Latin root given below. Write the word on the line, and then use it in a sentence.

1. *sens* means "be aware" _____

_____

_____

2. *sim* means "like" _____

_____

_____

3. *spec* means "see" _____

_____

_____

APPLY Choose a word from the box to complete each sentence. Each word contains the Latin root *sens, spec,* or *sim.* Write the word on the line.

assimilate	senseless	sensible	sensitive
simile	simulation	species	specific

4. Our neighbor acts tough, but he really is very _____ .

5. The story we read was about a(n) _____ crime that occurred long ago.

6. A(n) _____ type of tool was needed to put together the bookcase.

7. At the museum, there was a virtual reality _____ that people could try.

8. The immigrants are trying to _____ into the culture of their new country.

9. How does the _____ show a comparison between two things?

10. Be sure to eat a(n) _____ breakfast before school this morning.

11. The zoo is raising money for an endangered _____ .

Write a short paragraph using two or more words with a *sens/sim/spec* root.

12. _____

_____

_____

_____

Vocabulary

> **FOCUS** Review the selection vocabulary words from "A Year on Bowie Farm."

administered	reap
cull	retractable
hefted	rolling
intercept	romping
lush	scrabbling
operation	spigot

PRACTICE Read each sentence. Think about the meaning of the underlined word or words. Write the vocabulary word on the line that is similar in meaning.

1. We sat in the <u>thick, full</u> grass as we watched the parade.

_____

2. Connect the hose to the outdoor <u>faucet</u> and turn on the water.

_____

3. The gardener had to <u>reduce</u> the number of growing plants so the remaining ones would be stronger.

_____

4. The children were <u>jumping with excitement</u> around the playground.

_____

5. The farmers <u>harvest</u> the crops in early fall before it gets too cold.

_____

6. The nurse <u>provided</u> a flu vaccine to anyone who needed it.

_____

7. The chickens were <u>running frantically</u> when they sensed danger.

_____

8. The young man <u>worked hard to lift</u> the heavy bag onto the truck.

_____

9. We rode in the car over <u>rising and falling</u> hills on the long drive.

_____

10. The library has an efficient <u>way of working</u> to track books.

_____

11. We sat under the covering that was <u>able to be pulled back</u>.

_____

12. I need to <u>stop</u> the message about dinner since plans have changed.

_____

APPLY Read each question. Think about the meaning of the underlined vocabulary word. Write your answers on the line.

13. What might cause a dog to start <u>scrabbling</u> in the yard? _____

14. Where would you find a <u>spigot</u>? _____

15. What is something that you have <u>hefted</u>? _____

16. What is something you have seen that has a <u>retractable</u> part? _____

17. What is something that can be <u>administered</u> to students? _____

18. What might be in a <u>lush</u> garden? _____

Where History Lives

Have you ever heard of a living history museum? It is a special operation in which people dress like people did at a certain time in history. It can be a single operational farm in the rolling hills of the Midwest or it can be a whole village operating like it did hundreds of years ago in colonial America. When you step into this kind of museum, you can see the people, places, and things from that time. You can ask questions of the people who are working at the museum.

Imagine the living history museum looks like a small colonial village. Everyone will dress like the people who lived before the Revolutionary War in America. You may talk to a farmer who culls the apple tree to make sure it produces enough apples in the fall. The farmer will tell you about the hard work of plowing fields with animals. You could ask the farmer about what crops he reaps in the fall.

You could then step into the blacksmith's shop, who will show you how to make tools during this time. You may even see the blacksmith heft heavy iron into the fire and shape it into the tools needed by the farmer and other local residents of the colonial village. It might get hot in this shop, so you may wish to step into another shop, like the printmaker or the apothecary.

The printmaker's shop is an active place. Each letter of a paper or book is placed by hand on a large press. It might take over twenty-five hours to set all the letters for a one-page paper! During colonial times, this was where information was delivered and exchanged. You might ask if messages were ever intercepted by British soldiers or American patriots.

After the loud and active shops of the printmaker and blacksmith, take a walk in the lush garden of the apothecary. This is the place people would go if they did not feel well. The apothecary used the herbs from the garden to make and administer medicines and treatments for a variety of illnesses and injuries. What would you want to ask the apothecary?

Before you leave this colonial village, be sure to stop and talk to the many shop owners to discuss the many trades.

Now, step a hundred years into the future from the colonial village days and stop by a living historical farm of the 1880s. You see people in long sleeves and dresses, but in a simpler fashion than the colonial times. Instead of a village, all the people on the farm must depend on themselves and each other to do all the work.

As you enter the barn, the farmer will retract the heavy door and invite you inside to see the animals. In the spring, the barn is full of new life. You may see a lamb romp about the pen, and then scrabble out to the field to eat some fresh grass. You may see little piglets eating before they roll around in their muddy pen. Sometimes the farmer will ask you to help feed the chickens or collect the eggs!

Enter the outdoor kitchen, and you will notice there is no spigot for water. One of the people working in the kitchen might send you to the well to get some water. You soon realize it is not easy to heft a pail of water up the hill to the kitchen. When you hand the water to the woman cooking in the kitchen, you realize that half the water is gone! She suggests you help with other chores on the farm.

You find someone hefting heavy rugs onto ropes, and soon the person is beating the rugs. You help beat the rugs, and you knock clouds of dirt from them. Next, you help hang the heavy laundry on the line to dry. It seems like the chores of the farm will never end! The woman you are helping assures that you are correct—there is still much to do!

Once the housework is done, you wander to the garden and the fields. A farmer is plowing the fields with two large animals. Another is planting rows of vegetables near the house, and one person calls to you to help weed the garden. You help pull the weeds from the garden, which are all put together in a compost pile. The compost pile will eventually be used to fertilize plants.

After all this hard work, you see a swing hanging from a tree. You scrabble over to the swing and enjoy the timeless activity.

Apply Vocabulary • *Skills Practice 1*

Making Inferences

> **FOCUS** Readers get clues from the text and use their own prior knowledge to **make inferences** about characters and events in a story.

PRACTICE Read each sentence below. Make an inference about the character based on each sentence and write it on the line.

1. Rachel's heart beat fast as she grabbed the microphone and began singing.

   Inference: _____

2. Nick found a wallet on the ground, so he turned it into the police.

   Inference: _____

3. Chloe put on her uniform, laced up her shoes, and stepped onto the track.

   Inference: _____

4. Michael checked his phone, waited a few seconds and checked it again.

   Inference: _____

5. Melanie stood at the top of the high diving board and looked down at the pool.

   Inference: _____

6. Jack stepped up to the plate, held the bat ready, and stared at the pitcher.

   Inference: _____

APPLY Read the description of each character below. Then write a short paragraph describing how the character feels without actually stating it.

7. a student who is nervous about a test

_____

_____

_____

8. a movie star who is glamorous

_____

_____

_____

9. a cousin who is shy

_____

_____

_____

10. a brother or sister who is angry

_____

_____

_____

Access Complex Text • *Skills Practice 1*

Informational Writing

Think

Audience: Who will read your informational writing?

_____

Purpose: What is your reason for writing an informational text?

_____

Research and Note Taking

Paraphrasing means restating another person's words or ideas in your own words, often to make them shorter or simpler. You should paraphrase when you are taking notes or summarizing.

Plagiarism means copying someone else's words or ideas and passing them off as your own. Even if you rearrange the order of the author's sentences or paragraphs, it is still plagiarism. If you want to use someone's words or ideas, you must give them credit. Place quotes in quotation marks and list your sources in a bibliography.

Read the sample text from "One Small Step" by Vidas Barzdukas. Paraphrase the text on the lines. Then trade your paper with a partner to make sure you did not plagiarize the text.

Today, blasting a person into outer space is pretty unremarkable. In 1958, however, shooting a rocket into the sky proved nearly impossible. The first rocket for Project Mercury exploded on the launching pad. The second rocket flew only four inches off the ground before it crashed.

_____

_____

_____

_____

Revising

Use this checklist to revise your informational writing.

☐ Does the writing clearly introduce the topic?

☐ Does the writing have three paragraphs in the main body that share important details?

☐ Does the writing use precise, academic language?

☐ Does the writing use a variety of sentence types?

☐ Does the writing use transition words and phrases?

☐ Does the writing have an engaging conclusion that sums up the topic?

Editing/Proofreading

Use this checklist to correct mistakes in your informational writing.

☐ Did you use proofreading symbols when editing?

☐ Have you included commas where they are needed?

☐ Have compound sentences been punctuated correctly?

☐ Do all sentences end with the correct punctuation mark?

☐ Did you check the writing for misspelled words?

Publishing

Use this checklist to prepare your informational writing for publishing.

☐ Write or type a neat copy of your informational writing.

☐ Include a multimedia element to enhance the written information.

☐ Include a bibliography that cites sources used for research.

Latin Roots *sens*, *spec*, and *sim*

FOCUS Understanding and identifying **Latin roots** and their meanings can help you define and spell difficult and unfamiliar words. Here are some the Latin roots in the spelling words and their meanings:

sens = "feel"; *spec* = "see"; *sim* = "like"

PRACTICE Fill in the appropriate Latin root to form a spelling word.

Word List		Challenge Words:
1. assimilate	11. sensitive	1. desensitize
2. consensus	12. sensitivity	2. dissimilar
3. facsimile	13. sensory	3. simultaneous
4. inspect	14. simile	
5. inspector	15. simulate	
6. nonsense	16. simulator	
7. perspective	17. spectacle	
8. respect	18. spectator	
9. sensational	19. spectrum	
10. sensibility	20. speculate	

1. _____itivity

2. in_____tor

3. _____tator

4. _____ulate

5. _____itive

6. _____ulate

7. _____ibility

8. re_____t

9. _____ational

10. per_____tive

11. non_____e

12. con_____us

13. as_____ilate

14. _____ile

15. fac_____ile

16. _____ulator

17. _____tacle

18. _____ory

19. _____trum

20. in_____t

APPLY If the underlined spelling word is misspelled, write the correct spelling on the line. If the word is correct, then write *Correct* on the line.

21. That movie is a total <u>sinsery</u> experience. _____

22. You get an interesting <u>prespective</u> of the city as you fly over. _____

23. My drawing is not <u>disimilar</u> to yours. _____

24. An <u>inspecter</u> is coming to look at our house today. _____

25. Try to use a <u>simile</u> or metaphor in this paragraph. _____

26. Iona trusts her mother's <u>sinsibilty</u> about clothing. _____

27. Rohan will get to be a <u>specktator</u> at the inauguration. _____

28. The <u>consinsas</u> among my friends is that this song is great. _____

29. My brother's <u>nonsense</u> can be tiresome. _____

30. Dance class is held at a <u>symultanous</u> time as art class. _____

31. I have great <u>rispecked</u> for your hard work. _____

32. The girls <u>inspecked</u> their clothes for mud and grass stains. _____

Commas

> **FOCUS** **Commas** are used to organize the thoughts and items in a sentence. They show the reader where to pause so that a sentence's meaning can be clearly understood.
>
> - Use a comma to separate three or more items.
>
>   I eat bananas, apples, and oranges.
>
> - Use a comma after long introductory phrases or dependent clauses.
>
>   **After we finished cleaning the house,** my dad and I relaxed.
>
> - Use a comma and a conjunction to join two independent clauses in a compound sentence.
>
>   Luiz wants to play chess, **but** Shonda wants to play checkers.
>
> - Use a comma before or after a noun of direct address to set it off from the rest of the sentence.
>
>   **Lacy,** are you traveling to Kentucky this summer?
>
> - Use a comma to set off a tag question from the rest of the sentence.
>
>   The weather is beautiful today, **isn't it?**

PRACTICE The commas are missing or used incorrectly in the following sentences. Rewrite each sentence so that it is correct.

1. During our trip, to Texas we will drive through Tennessee, and Arkansas.

    _____

    _____

2. Hildy put on, a coat a hat a scarf and mittens and, then she went outside.

    _____

    _____

3. I usually like the author's books but, that story was pretty boring wasn't it?

_____

_____

4. When you get home Audrey you will remember, to let the dog out won't you?

_____

_____

5. We washed dried and peeled, the potatoes, before cutting them into pieces.

_____

_____

6. The band, played two ballads, two requested songs and one classical piece.

_____

_____

7. Before going to bed, we took showers brushed our teeth and turned out lights.

_____

_____

8. We went to a baseball game and TJ caught a foul ball.

_____

_____

APPLY Insert commas where they are needed in the paragraph.

You know that W. E. B. Du Bois was an important American civil rights leader don't you? He was also a writer poet editor and historian. Du Bois graduated from Harvard University in 1890 and then he studied in Europe for a few years. After returning to the United States Du Bois became the first black man to earn a Ph.D. from Harvard. Although he wrote many books Du Bois's most famous book was _The Souls of Black Folk._ He was also a founding member of the NAACP which stands for the National Association for the Advancement of Colored People. When Du Bois died in 1963 he was a citizen of Ghana.

Two Shots

  Eleven . . . The high-pitched sound made by ten pairs of squeaking tennis shoes permeates the hush that has fallen over the enormous crowd. *Ten . . .* Four players simultaneously leap into the air, one releasing the basketball that was perfectly perched upon her steady fingertips. *Nine . . .* The piercing trill of the referee's whistle resonates throughout the gymnasium.

  "Foul, number twenty-one, white team," shouts the referee. "Shooter is number thirty-two, red. Two shots." What a thrilling game this has proven to be! The Eagles, the home team wearing white, are winning by one point. The Wildcats, the visiting team draped in red, desperately need a miracle. A bench full of hopeful girls and a gymnasium full of anxious people wonder whether I have any miracles to spare.

  I, Callie Barton, am number thirty-two on the red team, the Wildcats. I am the player who was just fouled as she boldly attempted a game-winning jump shot. With nine seconds remaining, I have been allotted two free throws—the second of which could win the game and the conference championship for my team.

  "Time-out, white," calmly says the referee. This classic action in competitive sports is used when a player faces a high-pressure situation—a football kicker attempting a winning field goal or a basketball player attempting two free throws to win a game. In such situations, the opposing coach calls a time-out to give the player extra time to "think about it." The Eagles obviously expect me to crack under pressure.

  "Callie," whispers my coach, Mr. Himes. I see excitement in his eyes as he says, "Your team needs you to concentrate. Take this opportunity to put those practice shots to good use." When he mentions my "practice shots," he is referring to my famous tradition. I have this rule that I cannot leave the basketball court without making two free throws in a row, or I will suffer bad basketball luck. This routine often keeps me on the court after my teammates have gone home. My teammate Fran and I share rides, so she must wait for me on those evenings when I struggle. Her saying, "Come on, Cal! Sink those free throws so we can go home!" has practically become part of the tradition itself.

Once again, the referee's loud whistle sounds, signaling that the time-out has ended and play is to resume. Doubts begin parading through my mind as I approach the line. *If I miss the first attempt, I'm immediately a failure. Then, if I also miss the second shot, I am absolutely . . .*

"Cal!" Fran's enthusiastic voice startles me out of my own thoughts. As she claims her spot on the hash marks, she calmly assumes the rebounding position, smiles, and says, "Sink those free throws so we can go home!"

With those words, the simple truth of my situation is brought to light, and I finally recognize what Coach Himes and Fran have been suggesting with their words of encouragement. I can accomplish what I have to do right now simply because I accomplish it every day!

The referee flings the ball toward me, and I visualize myself on the free-throw line in my school's gym. I think about what I think about every night at the end of practice: *I've got to make my free throws. I wonder what Mom is making for dinner. What homework do I have to do?*

Swish! My first attempt glides across the air and slips through the basket. The roar of my teammates and our fans is exhilarating. As long as we prevent the Eagles from scoring, I have given my team another shot at victory in overtime.

Now I feel confident.

Swish! The second shot mimics the first. The Wildcats have reclaimed the lead with only nine seconds remaining.

Eight! . . . The Eagles quickly inbound the ball. *Seven* . . . My teammate Jill guards the opponent dribbling down the court. *Five* . . . The Eagle near Fran clutches the basketball. *Four* . . . She rotates and hurls a desperation shot. *Three* . . . It smacks the rim and bounces back out. *Two* . . . Fran grabs the rebound and clasps the basketball in her arms. *One* . . . BUZZ!

The Wildcats win! Everyone charges me, and I am instantly on the ground beneath a mound of celebration. Even my friends from the bleachers come to congratulate me and the other Wildcats. Once the excitement subsides, Fran announces, "I take back every time I teased you about your weird rule. Now let's go home—to celebrate!"

From Food to Fuel

You need energy to work, play, breathe, and even to read this sentence. Just like a car, your body must take in fuel and change it to energy so it can perform all its functions. That is where the digestive system comes in. The digestive system takes in fuel in the form of food, breaks it down, and sends it all around the body to be used as energy.

Sometimes when people think of digestion, they think only of the stomach. The stomach is one part of the system. But there are many parts and many steps to the process. Digestion starts with your teeth and your mouth. As you chew food, the saliva in your mouth immediately begins to break down the food. The saliva comes from special glands inside the head near the ear, tongue, and jaw. These glands are called salivary glands.

When you smell food cooking, the salivary glands start working. If you are hungry and catch a whiff of your favorite meal, before long your mouth may begin to water. As a matter of fact, you might even say digestion begins with the sense of smell!

Chewing breaks the food down into smaller and smaller pieces so it can be swallowed easily. The tongue also helps mash the food around in the mouth. Then the tongue pushes the food to the back of the throat and you swallow. When you swallow, the chewed-up food goes down a tube in the back of your throat called the esophagus. The windpipe, which receives the air you breathe in, also begins in the back of the throat. Your body has a special flap called the epiglottis that closes up the windpipe while you are swallowing and makes sure the food goes down the right tube. How does food then get down the esophagus? Muscles squeeze the walls of the esophagus, pushing the mashed food farther and farther down. After a few seconds, this squeezing motion has pushed the food down into the stomach.

The stomach is shaped like the letter *J*. It is sort of like a stretchy sack that expands when you eat a lot. Very strong stomach acids continue to digest the food even more. The food is churned in the stomach until it becomes a thick liquid. Now it is ready for the next step in the digestion process.

Next, the food enters another tube called the small intestine. It is very long and coiled around your insides below the stomach. If you stretched out an adult's small intestine, it would be around twenty feet long! The small intestine helps to break down food even more.

At this point, digestion gets help from some other organs in the body. The liver produces a substance called bile that helps break down fats so they can be absorbed into the bloodstream. Another organ, the pancreas, produces liquids that also help break down some nutrients. Food has now been reduced to microscopic pieces. It is a thin liquid by now, and as it travels through the walls of the small intestine, all those nutrients can be taken up by the bloodstream. The blood travels to every part of the body, supplying cells with these nutrients. But wait—there is more!

Next, the food that is not broken down and absorbed in the small intestine goes into the large intestine. The large intestine is not as long as the small intestine but still can stretch out to about five feet. That is as long as the average person is tall! The large intestine is filled with good bacteria that help break down food even more. The bacteria can be quite noisy when they are doing their job. Sometimes they bubble and make gas that your body releases as . . . well . . . gas. The large intestine also absorbs a lot of water while it holds the food your body does not use or need.

About eighteen to thirty hours after you eat something, the undigested food is ready to leave your body. The body has taken all the nutrients it can. Your food has been changed to fuel for riding your bike, playing soccer, or even doing your homework. The next morning, when you sit down to eat some cereal, the process of digestion begins once again.

Vocabulary

FOCUS Review the selection vocabulary words from "A Handful of Dirt."

churning	ratio
debris	ravenous
decay	ruthless
emit	succulents
excrete	supremacy
lubricated	

PRACTICE Complete each sentence with a selection vocabulary word. Each vocabulary word should be used once.

1. The waste that animals _____ from their bodies can be used to make the soil better.

2. The _____ from the strong windstorm could be found for miles.

3. You often find _____ in environments where it does not rain often, since they store water.

4. My brother is _____ when he plays games with me; he never lets me win.

5. The _____ of the runners will be determined in the upcoming championship race.

6. The dogs were _____ after playing and running outside for hours.

7. The strong winds were _____ the waves, which tossed the little boat on the sea.

8. The book to student _____ is ten to one, so there are ten books for every one student.

9. How long does it take an apple to _____ naturally on the ground?

10. When you blow a dog whistle, it will _____ a sound too high for the human ear to hear.

11. The _____ in the road will be repaired and sealed this week.

12. Jordan _____ the chains of the bicycle with oil before the bike ride.

APPLY Read each sentence. Answer each question by explaining the definition in your own words.

14. You are filling in the crevices in the patio with sand. What are you doing?

_____

15. The rescued kittens were ravenous when they were found. What does that mean?

_____

16. You lubricated the valves on your trumpet. What does that mean?

_____

17. The ratio of students to tables is two to one. What does that mean?

_____

18. The small flashlight will emit enough light to find the path. What is happening?

_____

Practice Vocabulary • *Skills Practice 1*

Choosing a King

Once upon a time, in a land far, far away, lived a prince named Frederick. His uncle was the King who had no children. The King would have to choose one of his nephews to follow him in ruling the kingdom. The King thought Frederick was too kind to be a good king. Frederick's brother Frank was known for his ruthlessness. Frank always boasted about his supremacy to all in the royal court. Frank did not seem to care what others thought of him, and the King admired that.

One night the King dreamed that his kingdom was decaying. All the plants were dying, and even the succulents in the area were without water! The people were ravenous because nothing would grow and there was so little to eat. He was not sure what he could do as King to help the people of his country. His dream showed that Frank was King, and he suddenly awoke.

The following day, the King's mind churned with thoughts of the dream, trying to understand its meaning. He tried to shake the bad feeling of the dream, but he could not. He thought it might be a warning that Frank would not make a good king, but he still felt Frederick was too gentle to be a good king. What could he do? Maybe Frederick needed to do some hard work. So, the King ordered Frederick to help the town folk clear out the debris from a recent storm. Frederick was glad to do his part to help the people.

Frederick worked hard, chopping up large trees that had fallen across the road. He worked from sunrise to sunset, developing calluses on his hands from all the hard work. Frederick liked the hard work, he liked working alongside the people, and he liked knowing that his work helped others. Frank saw how people liked Frederick, and soon he had a ruthless plan to keep Frederick from becoming king.

"Brother, you have been working so hard and your hands must be blistered and callused. You must try this ointment," said Frank as he handed Frederick the small jar of cream. "Just use a ratio of one spoonful of ointment to three drops of oil for three days, and you will never have another callus again!"

"Thank you, Brother," said Frederick, "It is kind of you to think of me."

Skills Practice 1 • Apply Vocabulary

Frederick knew his brother was ruthless and not someone who thought of others first. So, he decided not to use the ointment Frank gave him, even though he hands were sore from all the work. Perhaps he would ask some of the people in town what they did.

When he asked the man chopping the tree next to him, the man emitted a loud laugh. Frederick was surprised at that response. The man said that his hands had been hard with calluses since he was a young boy. He explained that any lubricating cream would just make the hands soft and they would hurt longer. He just needed to let the skin harden, and it would not hurt.

Frederick thanked the man and got back to work chopping and breaking down the debris that littered the town. As he worked, he wondered what he should do with the jar of ointment. It obviously wasn't anything he would need, but what could he do with it? It might have something dangerous in it, like some sort of poison excreted from a frog, but it would be impossible to know for sure.

After a few weeks, the debris was clear from the town and the King ordered Frederick back to the royal court. He wanted to speak with both Frederick and Frank about the future of the kingdom. During the last few weeks, he thought about the qualities that made a good king, and he was starting to rethink which nephew would be the best king. Frederick proved tough, in addition to being kind, and Frank had continued to be ruthless and self-serving.

Frank and Frederick appeared before the king, giving their respects for his supremacy. The King surprised them by saying, "I have a bad blister on my hand. Would either of you have a healing ointment I could use?"

Frederick pulled out the jar of ointment that Frank had given him. Frank's eyes grew wide, recognizing it at once, and said, "No, brother! This is not for the King!"

"Why not?" asked the King, "Did you not give this ointment to your brother to heal his blisters?"

"I did, your majesty," started Frank, "however if you use it, all that you touch will decay."

The King knew at once the meaning of his dream and that Frederick would be the next king.

Apply Vocabulary • *Skills Practice 1*

Cause and Effect

FOCUS
- A **cause** is the reason an event happens.
- An **effect** is what happens as a result of a cause.

The words *because, since, therefore,* and *so* show the reader that a cause-and-effect relationship has taken place.

PRACTICE Complete each cause-and-effect relationship below by providing the missing half.

1. The path was steep and slippery, so _____

_____

2. Isaiah won the local spelling bee, so _____

_____

3. Because the runner did not give up, _____

_____

4. The family packed their belongings in boxes because _____

_____

APPLY Read the sentences below, and identify the cause and effect in each one.

5. We have no school today because it is a holiday.

Effect: _____

Cause: _____

6. Because the baby was tired and hungry, he cried and cried.

Effect: _____

Cause: _____

7. I wanted to know more about butterflies, so I did some reading and research.

Effect: _____

Cause: _____

8. Jack cleaned his room because it was messy and he could not find his homework.

Effect: _____

Cause: _____

9. I do not like mushrooms in my salad, so I did not eat them.

Effect: _____

Cause: _____

10. I am going to the airport because my aunt's plane just landed.

Effect: _____

Cause: _____

Access Complex Text • *Skills Practice 1*

Prefix *inter-*; Suffixes *-ish, -ism*; Greek root *chron*

> **FOCUS** The prefix *inter-* means "between" or "among." For example, the word *interact* means "to act between" or "to talk to or do things with others."
>
> The suffix *-ish* means "near," "like," or "almost." Adding *-ish* to a word creates an adjective. For example, the word *child* becomes *childish,* meaning "like a child."
>
> The suffix *-ism* means "state of" or "quality of." Adding *-ism* to a word creates a noun. For example, the word *athletic* becomes *athleticism,* meaning "quality of being athletic."
>
> The Greek word *chron* means "time." For example, the word *chronic* means "relating to time," or in other words, "for a long period of time."

PRACTICE Add *inter-, -ish,* or *-ism* to each base word below to create a real word. Then write the new word's definition.

1. _____state

_____

2. _____national

_____

3. hero_____

_____

4. fool_____

_____

APPLY Each word contains the prefix *inter-*, the suffixes *-ish*, or *-ism*, or the Greek root *chron*. Choose the word that fits the definition and write it on the line and then use it in a sentence.

chronograph	interconnected	internet	patriotism
pinkish	sevenish	tourism	synchronized

5. state of touring _____

_____

_____

6. quality of a patriot _____

_____

_____

7. near seven _____

_____

_____

8. connected between _____

_____

_____

9. made to happen at the same time _____

_____

_____

10. an instrument used for measuring time _____

_____

_____

Vocabulary

FOCUS Review the selection vocabulary words from "Island Treasures: Growing Up in Cuba."

arrogant   nostalgia
authoritarian   prevalent
formal   remote
formidable   steadfast
manufacturer

PRACTICE Complete each sentence with a selection vocabulary word. Each vocabulary word should be used once.

1. Because of our _____ friendship, we have shared many years of tears and laughter.

2. The _____ opinion of the community is that we should continue the yearly festival.

3. The dinner will be _____ so you will need to wear a suit and tie.

4. It will be difficult to travel to the _____ village in the mountains.

5. Our father formed a set of _____ rules at home, so we do what he says.

6. Grandpa had moments of _____ as he walked into the house where he grew up.

7. My _____ teammate thought she knew best about every aspect of the sport.

8. I contacted the _____ to get the instruction manual since we could not find one in the house.

9. That team is a _____ opponent—they have won every game this season!

APPLY Look at the word in italics. Which option is the best match? Write your answer and then an explanation on the line below.

10. *formal:* a tuxedo or a jersey? _____

Why? _____

11. *remote:* a cabin in the wilderness or a house in a village? _____

Why? _____

12. *prevalent:* books at a library or books at a playground? _____

Why? _____

13. *formidable:* an easy assignment or a big school presentation? _____

Why? _____

14. *steadfast:* a trusted family member or a new neighbor? _____

Why? _____

Practice Vocabulary • *Skills Practice 1*

A New Program

On Friday, our teacher told us that Mrs. Sullivan, our principal, would be meeting with all the fifth grade classes to discuss a new program she wants to begin at our school. Mrs. Sullivan wanted us to know that we would be an integral part of the program and its success. Although Mrs. Sullivan held the position of authority in our school, she never seemed like a strict authoritarian. She had a warmth and flexibility in her leadership style. So, we were excited to hear more from her about this new program.

The next week, Mrs. Sullivan came to our classroom to tell us about her program, Kindergarten Buddies. She greeted us, "Good morning! I would like to start a buddy program here at the school to manufacture a strong feeling of community and connectedness among our students. I want you to think back to your kindergarten year, and then imagine the fifth graders you saw in the hallway. How did they look?"

Hands shot up in the air and Mrs. Sullivan called on a few students to share what they remembered: "The fifth graders looked so huge!" "The fifth graders seemed to live in a very remote part of the school, far from our kindergarten classroom." "I was a little afraid of them because they seemed so giant."

Mrs. Sullivan nodded, and then replied, "As a fifth grader, you will be assigned a kindergarten buddy. You will begin by formally introducing yourself and then you will do a short activity together. The goal is to break down the formidable image of the fifth graders and to develop a steadfast friendship over the year. The fifth grade teachers will work with the kindergarten teachers to pair up students."

"Now, as fifth graders, I have high expectations for you. I expect you to be role models of proper behavior for your kindergarten partners—being good listeners when you are given instructions and following those directions. I expect you to be thoughtful and kind buddies during your time together. I know you will," finished Mrs. Sullivan. "Do you have any questions about the program?"

"Mrs. Sullivan, when will we find out who our buddy will be? You know I will be the best buddy of the entire fifth grade," Kevin finished, almost arrogantly.

Mrs. Sullivan smiled and answered, "I am sure you will. We will start next month."

In preparation for our visit, we practiced formally introducing ourselves to a partner: "Hello, I am Maria. I am in Mr. Allen's fifth grade class. How are you?" We practiced asking some basic questions about what our buddies like best about school and what they are learning. Then, Mr. Allen gave us the name of our kindergarten buddy and asked us to write a short note to our buddy on a blank postcard he gave us.

I looked at the name Mr. Allen gave me, Julia Alvarez, and then I began writing my note. I told Julia that I had an older brother and a younger sister, as well as a dog named Max. I told her how much I loved the monkey bars on the playground. I finished the note telling her how excited I was to meet her, and I drew a picture of my family, including Max. Later that week, I received a picture from Julia that showed a girl with a large smile on her face that simply said "Julia."

Two weeks later, we lined up to go to the kindergarten classroom where we would meet our kindergarten buddy for the first time. As we walked into the kindergarten classroom, I was suddenly hit with memories of kindergarten. I had forgotten the prevalence of bright colors in the decorations of the room, from the carpet to the posters on the walls. I looked nostalgically at the stacks of games on one shelf, the picture books on display, and the teaching clock along one wall of the room. I remember how proud I was when I finally mastered these skills, which seem so easy now.

The teachers helped us find our kindergarten buddy, and I soon introduced myself to Julia. Then, the kindergarten teacher clapped her hands in rhythm, and the children clapped the rhythm in response. I remotely remembered my kindergarten teacher clapping to us so long ago, and it made me smile at the nostalgic thought. We played a question game to learn more about each other.

Julia and I found that we had much in common. We both had an older brother and a younger sister. We both loved to tell stories. Throughout the year, we wrote steadfastly to each other, sharing funny stories, especially those involving arrogant older brothers! I think this program was a success.

Apply Vocabulary • *Skills Practice 1*

Fact and Opinion

> **FOCUS** Good writers use both facts and opinions in their writing. A good reader can tell one from the other.
>
> - **Facts** are details that can be proven true or false.
> - **Opinions** are what people think. They cannot be proven true or false.

PRACTICE Read each sentence below and tell whether it is a fact or an opinion.

1. Alma Flor Ada tells the most beautiful stories. _____

2. Alma Flor Ada was born in Cuba. _____

3. Tadpoles turn into frogs. _____

4. It was hard to find a bull frog on the farm. _____

5. River turtles live in the stream by the fields. _____

6. A fallen tree looks like a shipwreck. _____

7. The fish in the stream eat mosquito larvae. _____

8. Alma's grandfather told many stories. _____

9. Alma's grandfather was a great storyteller. _____

10. Orange blossoms smell wonderful in the spring. _____

APPLY Write one fact and one opinion you have about each topic below. Use complete sentences.

11. a farm animal

Fact: _____

Opinion: _____

12. an author

Fact: _____

Opinion: _____

13. a parade

Fact: _____

Opinion: _____

14. Cuba

Fact: _____

Opinion: _____

Copyright © McGraw-Hill Education

Narrative Writing

Think

Audience: Who will read your narrative writing?

_____

Purpose: What is your reason for writing a narrative?

_____

PREWRITING Write a short description of an experience you had or read about in which a lesson was learned. Use the topic ideas below to help you.

a lesson about fairness

a lesson about responsibility

a lesson about following rules

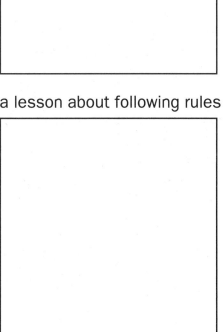

a lesson about safety

PREWRITING Use this character web to organize the traits of your main character. Write the character's name in the middle. Then write one of the character's traits in each of the small circles. Finally, list behaviors that demonstrate each trait in the bigger circles.

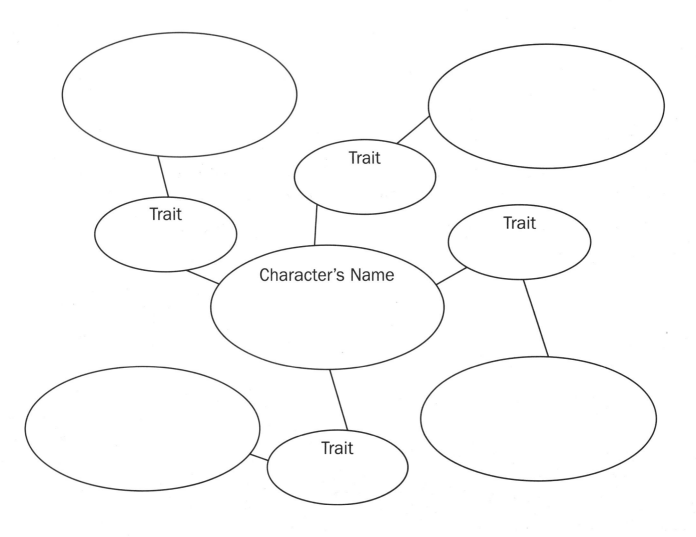

Prefix *inter-*, Suffixes *-ish* and *-ism*, Greek Root *chron*

FOCUS Identifying Greek roots, prefixes, and suffixes and their meanings can help you spell difficult words.

- The **Greek root *chron*** means "time."
- The **prefix *inter-*** means "among" or "between."
- The **suffix *-ish*** means "near," "like," or "almost." It creates an adjective when added to a base word.
- The **suffix *-ism*** means "state or quality of." It creates a noun when added to a base word.

PRACTICE Add the suffix *-ish* or *-ism* or the root *chron* to the following word parts to create a spelling word.

Word List

1. bookish
2. chronic
3. chronicle
4. chronological
5. chronometer
6. criticism
7. feverish
8. foolish
9. interject
10. intermediate
11. interruption
12. intersperse
13. intertwine
14. mannerism
15. optimism
16. organism
17. stylish
18. symbolism
19. synchronize
20. ticklish

Challenge Words

1. amateurish
2. anachronism
3. metabolism

1. fool_____

2. tickl_____

3. _____ject

4. symbol_____

5. styl_____

6. critic_____

7. _____twine

8. _____icle

9. optim_____

10. _____ruption

11. syn_____ize

12. fever_____

13. _____ometer

14. _____ic

APPLY On the line, write the spelling word that is related by a common root or base word to each of the following words.

15. organic _____

16. illogical _____

17. symbolic _____

18. rejection _____

19. millimeter _____

20. tickled _____

21. restyling _____

22. mediation _____

23. corrupting _____

24. critical _____

25. ill-mannered _____

26. notebook _____

27. dispersed _____

28. optimal _____

Complex Sentences

> ## FOCUS
> A complex sentence contains an independent clause and one or more dependent clauses.
>
> - An **independent clause** stands alone as a sentence.
>
>   *I found the book in the fiction section.*
>
> - A **dependent clause** has a subject and a verb, but it cannot stand alone as a sentence. Many dependent clauses begin with subordinating conjunctions.
>
>   *I found the book in the fiction section **after I asked the librarian for help**.*
>
> - When a dependent clause begins a sentence, a comma is used to separate it from the independent clause.
>
>   ***Although I thought it was a true story,** I found the book in the fiction section.*

PRACTICE
Label each sentence with a **C** if it is a complex sentence or **X** if it is not a complex sentence.

1. _____ After Aziza finishes working on the computer, she logs out before turning off the power.

2. _____ The lights dimmed because the movie was about to begin.

3. _____ Maya's uncle always brings news about friends and relatives in Dallas.

4. _____ The sheriff told the posse to head out while the sun still shone, and then he walked back inside the building.

5. _____ Before Paul finishes writing his novel, he hopes to find a publisher.

APPLY Underline the independent clause and circle the dependent clause in each sentence.

6. After Jim's mom dropped us off, we headed to English class.

7. As the bus was pulling away, Jeremy ran out of his house to the bus stop.

8. Because the Shamrocks won the softball game, the entire town had a big celebration.

9. The dog tried to run away whenever he thought he was getting a bath.

10. Matt liked to sleep in during the summer unless his grandfather was going to let him ride the tractor.

Combine each set of clauses below to create a complex sentence. Be sure to use one of the subordinating conjunctions from the box.

so	because	unless	whenever

11. it's cold enough; my friend Donyell likes to ice skate

_____

_____

12. Angelo studied at the library yesterday; it was much quieter

_____

_____

13. a special visitor was coming for dinner; I helped clean the house

_____

_____

14. Krista finds the map; she won't know the way to the reunion

_____

_____

Grammar • *Skills Practice 1*

Latin Roots *vac, grad/gress;* Greek Root *meter*

FOCUS Greek and Latin roots are common in the English language. Identifying and understanding roots can help you define difficult and unfamiliar words. When you know the meaning of a root, you can determine the meanings of many words that contain that root.

The Latin root *vac* means "empty." For example, the word *vacate* means "to empty" or "to leave." The Latin root *grad/gress* means "step" or "go." For example, the word *gradual* means "having characteristics of steps" or "changing in small steps" and the word *progress* means "going forward."

The Greek root *meter* means "measure." For example, the word *speedometer* means "an instrument that measures speed."

PRACTICE Think of a word that uses each Greek or Latin root given. Write the word on the line, and then use it in a sentence.

1. *vac* means "empty" _____

_____

2. *grad* means "step" or "go" _____

_____

3. *gress* means "step" or "go" _____

_____

4. *meter* means "measure" _____

_____

APPLY Choose a word from the box to complete each sentence. Each word contains the Latin roots *vac* or *grad/gress*, or the Greek root *meter*. Write the word on the line.

congress	grade	pedometer	progress
thermometer	upgrade	vacant	vacuum

5. Next year, I will be in sixth _____ at school.

6. The animal conservation organization held a(n) _____ to discuss important topics.

7. Dad used the _____ to clean up the mess under the table.

8. A(n) _____ helps walkers and runners measure the distance they go.

9. It was time to _____ the toddler's bed from a crib to a twin bed.

10. After a losing season last year, the team has won five games and is making

    great _____.

11. The city has decided to turn the _____ lot into a space for a farmer's market.

12. The nurse used a(n) _____ to check the patient's temperature.

Vocabulary

FOCUS Review the selection vocabulary words from "The Pot That Juan Built."

battled	potsherds
calico	prize
cherishes	reflect
fashioned	solitude
impoverished	supplemented
patrons	windswept

PRACTICE Read each sentence. Write the vocabulary word on the line that best completes each sentence.

1. If you find broken pieces of ceramic, these pieces are called _____.

2. When a place has an obvious lack of resources, it is _____.

3. If you add to your knowledge by reading outside of class, you _____ the information you knew.

4. When the two teams fought for the championship, they _____ for a victory.

5. If your grandfather likes to sit alone in the garden, he enjoys his

   _____.

6. If you choose a cat with spots of different colors, describe its coat as

   _____.

7. When the wind whips your hair into a messy style, you can say it is your

_____ look.

8. When a girl loves and cares for her pet, she _____ it.

9. If several individuals donate money to support the museum, they are

_____.

10. If scientists think carefully about the results they see, they _____ on their observations.

11. If the two boys value the autographed ball, they _____ it.

12. If you make a raincoat out of a garbage bag, you _____ the bag into a raincoat.

APPLY Read each question. Think about the meaning of the underlined vocabulary word. Write your answers on the lines.

13. How would you feel if someone <u>cherishes</u> you?

_____

14. How could <u>patrons</u> support a local concert series?

_____

15. Where might you go if you wanted <u>solitude</u>?

_____

16. Where might you find a <u>windswept</u> place?

_____

17. What is something that you <u>prize</u>?

_____

18. Why might you <u>reflect</u> on a conversation?

_____

Practice Vocabulary • *Skills Practice 1*

Upcycled Art

On Saturday, Lucas and his family went to the local flea market. He loved to look at the many booths and reflect on the assorted items available for sale. He especially liked finding artists selling upcycled items. Artists who specialized in upcycling reused items and made them look beautiful. The artists upcycled various materials, including old clothing, tin cans, glass jars, potsherds, and silverware.

Lucas and his family meandered through the market. They saw calico shirts fashioned into rugs, globes fashioned into lights, and potsherds fashioned into jewelry. Sometimes, they would find an artist working on a piece while patrons studied the finished products. The artist would supplement the old item with something new, such as a bead or some paint to create something wonderfully different. Lucas was amazed at the imagination of the artists.

One artist specialized in repurposing old T-shirts into a variety of items. Some T-shirts transformed into pillows, while others changed into tote bags. The artist also created new items by weaving parts of T-shirts together. Some were small, like key chains or headbands. The most impressive items were large multi-colored rugs, which must have contained hundreds of T-shirts.

Artists from an impoverished area created magnets from found objects. They made magnets from bottle caps painted to look like lady bugs. They formed flower magnets from solitary earrings missing their match. They supplemented the magnet backing with an assortment of game pieces, keyboard keys, and buttons and displayed them on a magnetic board. The artists even created magnets from discarded tops of tin cans. They artfully positioned maps and printed paper on lids with small magnets on the back.

One artist upcycled utensils, transforming forks and spoons into new functional and decorative objects. Some forks were bent to create hooks on a piece of wood. Some forks were bent with the pointed end up so it could hold photos or prized recipes on small cards. Lucas was most amazed by the jewelry fashioned by bending the pointed ends into curving lines. These pieces took the shape of elephants, flowers, and even an octopus!

Lucas and his family discovered more treasures in the upcycled booths at the flea market. He reflected on items he had at home. How could he make a cherished item from discarded things? Later at home, Lucas began thinking in solitude for something he could create.

Lucas looked at his most prized possessions. He had a collection of seashells from the beach near his house. He had a collection of ribbons and medals he won in academic contests. His most cherished ribbon was the large blue one he received in the Battle of the Books contest, where he won first place for reading the most books over the summer. What could he make from seashells or ribbons?

He looked more closely at his found beach treasures, which he kept in an old shoebox. There were shells of all different sizes and shapes. He recalled the windswept beach where he found most of these items, with the large dunes separating the beach from the houses. He remembered battling the winds coming off the water as he looked carefully in the sand for new shells. The memories made him smile as he imagined ways to remake these found items.

He could remake the old shoebox into something more beautiful to hold his special treasures. Or, he could use the seashells and ribbons to decorate a picture frame or scrapbook. He reflected on the items he saw at the flea market: magnets, pillows, and jewelry. He could also make a clock or a decorative vase with his cherished items. Then, he heard the distant sound of a wind chime from outside.

Lucas could fashion a wind chime using his medals, seashells, and ribbons! He would need to supplement his collection with some string and something strong at the top. He found a few small sticks from the beach, which he tied together. He cut some of his smaller ribbons into strips to make a colorful string. He cut them thin enough so he could string the shells onto them.

Lucas needed holes in the shells so he could string them on the cut ribbons. He asked his dad for help drilling holes into the shells. Once the holes were in place, he strung the shells on the string. He then tied his medals to the bottoms of each string of shells. He attached the string of shells and medal to the top so it would swing in the wind. He finished the wind chime by adding his cherished blue ribbon at the top and then held it up. He smiled as he hung his wind chime outside.

Apply Vocabulary • *Skills Practice 1*

Sequence

> **FOCUS** The **sequence** in which events occur in a story is indicated by time words and order words.

PRACTICE Read each sentence. Write the time and order word or phrase in each sentence on the line.

1. We eat dinner at 6:30 every evening.

    _____

2. Meet me at the front of the school before the first bell rings.

    _____

3. Then, we can walk to class together.

    _____

4. We waited all day for the announcement of the winners.

    _____

5. We will go to Texas and visit our family in December.

    _____

6. The next step in building the shelter is adding leaves to the frame.

    _____

7. I pack my lunch every day.

    _____

8. I was happy that I reached my goal at last!

    _____

APPLY Read each paragraph below. Then, rewrite the events in the paragraph in the correct sequence.

9. Then, replace the lid as a nose and add eyes, feet, and a tail. It is easy to fashion a piggy bank from a milk jug. Finally, find the perfect place to place your new bank so it can collect some money. First, rinse out the milk jug with water and set the lid aside for later. Next, paint the clean milk jug pink. Once the paint is dry, turn the jug on its side and cut a slit on the new top.

_____

_____

_____

_____

_____

_____

10. At noon, we started the laundry and picked up the house. In the morning, we worked in the flower garden. We were tired by the evening, but we still put our clothes away. In the afternoon, we cleaned the bathroom and washed the floors. We spent all day Saturday working around our home.

_____

_____

_____

_____

_____

_____

Access Complex Text • *Skills Practice 1*

Narrative Writing

Revising

Point of view is the perspective from which a story is being told. A story written in first-person point of view is told by a character in the story. The narrator (the person telling the story) will use personal pronouns, such as *I, my, mine, us, we, ours,* and *our.* A story written in third-person point of view is told by a narrator who is not a character in the story. Personal pronouns appear only in dialogue when spoken by characters in the story.

It is important to maintain a consistent point of view in a story. If you switch from first person to third person, or vice versa, you will confuse your readers. The paragraph below has an inconsistent point of view. Rewrite the paragraph to correct the inconsistency.

When the students arrived at the zoo, I ran straight over to the duck pond. He put a quarter into the duck food dispenser, and the ducks began quickly swimming toward me. As he tossed the duck food into the air, a huge gust of wind came rolling over the pond. The dry bits of duck lunch blasted right back into his face. That's how I found out what duck food tastes like!

_____

_____

_____

_____

_____

_____

_____

Revising

Use this checklist to revise your narrative writing.

☐ Does the story introduce the main character and problem at the beginning?

☐ Is it clear where and when the story takes place?

☐ Does the story have rising action in the middle?

☐ Does the story develop the main character?

☐ Does the story have a climax?

☐ Does the writing have a consistent point of view?

☐ Does the writing have a strong voice?

☐ Is it clear that the story is realistic fiction?

Editing/Proofreading

Use this checklist to correct mistakes in your narrative writing.

☐ Did you use proofreading symbols when editing?

☐ Did you check for mistakes in complex sentences?

☐ Did you check for correct use of participles and participial phrases?

☐ Did you check the writing for misspelled words?

☐ Did you check the writing for mistakes in capitalization?

Publishing

**Use this checklist to prepare your narrative writing
for publishing.**

☐ Write or type a neat copy of the narrative writing.

☐ Add a cover page with a title and visual element related to the story.

Latin Roots *vac* and *grad/gress;* Greek Root *meter*

FOCUS Understanding and identifying **Latin** and **Greek roots** and their meanings can help you define and spell difficult and unfamiliar words. Here are some of the roots in the spelling words and their meanings.

Latin root **vac** = "empty;" Latin roots **grad/gress** = "step" or "go"; Greek root **meter** = "measure"

PRACTICE Add the missing root, prefix, or suffix to each base word or word part to form a spelling word.

Word List		Challenge Words
1. aggressive	11. regress	1. biodegradable
2. barometer	12. retrograde	2. vacillate
3. degrade	13. symmetry	3. odometer
4. diameter	14. thermometer	
5. evacuee	15. upgrade	
6. geometry	16. vacancy	
7. graduation	17. vacant	
8. millimeter	18. vaccinate	
9. perimeter	19. vacuous	
10. progression	20. vacuum	

1. _____ant

2. thermo_____

3. up_____e

4. re_____

5. sym_____y

6. _____uous

7. pro _____ion

8. _____cinate

9. milli_____

10. de_____e

11. ag_____ive   14. peri_____

12. baro_____   15. _____ancy

13. retro_____   16. _____uation

APPLY Circle the correctly spelled word in each pair.

17. vacancy   vacency

18. graduation   gradeution

19. agresive   aggressive

20. diameter   diamiter

21. evacee   evacuee

22. pragresion   progression

23. odomitter   odometer

24. vacume   vacuum

25. vacsanate   vaccinate

26. symmetry   simitry

27. thermometer   theromitter

28. millimeter   milameter

29. retragrade   retrograde

30. geometry   goemetery

Participial Phrases

FOCUS
- A **participle** is a verb that acts as an adjective.

    Jacob **stacked** the books. (*stacked* tells the action of the subject, *Jacob*)

    The books **stacked** on the table are going back to the library. (*stacked* is a participle modifying the noun *books*)

- A **participial phrase** includes the participle and other words in the phrase that modify a noun or pronoun.

    The books **stacked on the table** are going back to the library.

- A participial phrase must be next to the noun or pronoun it modifies. A misplaced participial phrase can change the meaning of a sentence.

    Riding on the train, Ava saw a farm with lots of cows. (modifies *Ava*)

    Ava saw a farm with lots of cows **riding on the train**. (modifies *cows*)

PRACTICE Circle each participle and underline each participial phrase.

1. That old house standing at the corner of Broad and Main will be torn down.

2. Anything piled in that box can be taken to the resale shop located downtown.

3. Ms. Reynolds has an aquarium filled with tropical fish.

4. Playing in front of an audience for the first time, Samuel felt strangely calm.

APPLY Add a participial phrase to each sentence below.

5. Those paintbrushes need to be cleaned.

_____

_____

6. The pizza has tomato sauce, cheese, and pepperoni.

_____

_____

7. Theo walked out the library's door.

_____

_____

8. Our trip to New York was canceled.

_____

_____

Rewrite each sentence to make its meaning clear.

9. Walking outside into the humid air, her glasses became foggy.

_____

_____

10. The chicken is in the coop laying an egg.

_____

_____

Suffixes *-ous/-eous/-ious*; Greek Root *onym*

FOCUS The suffixes *-ous/-eous/-ious* mean "possessing the qualities of." These suffixes create adjectives. For example, the word *humor* becomes an adjective, *humorous,* meaning "possessing the qualities of humor."

The Greek root *onym* means "name." For example, the word *anonymous* means "without a name."

PRACTICE Write the word from the box that matches each definition below.

acronym	courageous	glorious
outrageous	repetitious	studious

1. possessing the qualities of courage _____

2. possessing the qualities of studying _____

3. a word formed using the first letter of each word in a phrase _____

4. possessing the qualities of glory _____

5. possessing the qualities of outrage or anger _____

6. possessing the qualities of repeating _____

APPLY Complete the "word-math" problems below by combining the base word and suffix or the prefix and root and writing the word on the line. Then use each word in a sentence.

7. fury + ous = _____

_____

_____

8. adventure + ous = _____

_____

_____

9. syn + onym = _____

_____

_____

10. nausea + ous = _____

_____

_____

11. hilarity + ious = _____

_____

_____

12. extra + eous= _____

_____

_____

13. anti + onym = _____

_____

_____

14. advantage + ous = _____

_____

_____

Word Analysis • *Skills Practice 1*

Vocabulary

> **FOCUS** Review the selection vocabulary words from "Heading Home."

attendant	excursion
authentic	kabob
awnings	suburbs
candlelight	subtle
croissant	trekked
dormitory	waterfront

PRACTICE Read each sentence. Think about the meaning of the underlined word or words. Write the vocabulary word on the line that is similar in meaning.

1. The photographer <u>made a long journey on foot</u> up the mountain to take some amazing pictures.

   _____

2. My cousin lives in the <u>residential area just outside the city</u> on the east side.

   _____

3. The <u>flaky pastry shaped like a crescent moon</u> tasted buttery and delicious.

   _____

4. The <u>person whose job is to provide assistance</u> at the coat check took our coats at the theater.

   _____

5. The college student went back to the <u>building at her school used for housing</u> so she could sleep.

   _____

6. The magician used a <u>stealthy</u> hand movement to trick the audience.

   _____

7. The best food at the festival was a <u>stick with seasoned roasted meat and vegetables</u>.

_____

8. People sat under the restaurant's <u>canvas roofs</u> so they could enjoy the shade.

_____

9. She walked along the <u>section of town bordering the water</u> and looked at the boats.

_____

10. We had dinner by <u>the mild light provided only by candles</u> when the electricity went out.

_____

11. The <u>short trip taken for fun</u> to the wildlife park took three hours.

_____

12. The name-brand bag was <u>real and genuine</u> and not a fake, like I thought at first.

_____

APPLY **Read each question. Think about the meaning of the underlined vocabulary word. Write your answer on the line.**

13. Where might you find an <u>attendant</u> to help you? _____

14. What are some things you might see on the <u>waterfront</u>? _____

15. What kind of sandwiches might be made with a <u>croissant</u>? _____

16. What is a <u>subtle</u> way to let someone know you agree? _____

17. If you could go on an <u>excursion</u> for the day, where would you go? _____

18. How can you tell if something is <u>authentic</u> or not? _____

Practice Vocabulary • *Skills Practice 1*

A Cultural Camp

Growing up in the suburbs, Ava longed to visit the city and to travel to different places around the world. She wanted to hear authentic music from different countries and taste authentically prepared ethnic foods. Her parents were uninterested in traveling far from home, so she had to imagine what these places might be like. When Ava's suburban neighbors returned from visiting a foreign country, she would pepper them with questions about the people, houses, music, and most of all the food.

When Ava went to the library to check out more books about world cultures, she saw a poster on the community bulletin board. It said "Travel the World in One Week! A Special Experience for Students!" As she read more, she learned that the students stay in dormitories at a campus in the city. Each day, the students will attend classes and go on excursions to explore a variety of cultures. Now, how could she subtly let her parents know about this summer experience?

Ava wrote down the website listed on the poster and when she returned home, she typed in the web address and the same heading popped up in the window. She left it on the screen and went to go make sure her chores were finished. The screen went dark and her mother walked by without even looking. Maybe her initial plan was too subtle.

Ava brought up the web page again just before her mother went to work on the bills. Her mother continued to look through the bills while the computer screen went dark again. Ava decided to forget subtleness, and just ask directly. "Hey, mom," Ava started, "I saw this great summer camp where I could experience world cultures. Would I be able to go?"

Ava explained all she learned from the website and the poster. She shared that she would stay in the dormitory with other students, go to classes on campus, and then go on excursions every day. Her mother said that they would have to talk to her father and do a little more research into the program. They would discuss it further when they had more information.

The next week, Ava's parents said she could attend if she earned some money to help pay her way. Her father suggested that she could be an attendant at the gym.

Ava followed her father's suggestion and worked as an attendant at the local gym. She was glad to go to work, knowing that the money she earned would go toward her summer experience. She liked meeting all the patrons of the gym, checking them in and answering their questions. After a few months, she was helping to train the new attendants.

The rest of the school year went by quickly, and Ava grew more excited about going to campus for the world culture experience. She was a little nervous about staying overnight in the dormitory until she received the name of her summer dormitory roommate, Makayla. Soon, they were writing back and forth and sharing ideas about what the classes and excursions would be like.

The week finally arrived, and Ava arrived at the dormitory with her parents on Sunday at the same time as Makayla. Their parents helped them unpack, make the bed, and get settled. As soon as they had her area set up, the two families decided to walk along the waterfront park nearby. After their walk, Ava and Makayla returned to the dormitory, met their counselor, and said goodbye to their parents. They talked until lights out, and finally got some rest.

The next morning, the counselor greeted Ava and Makayla, leading them to their first class. It was a trek to the first class, almost a mile of walking across the campus from the dormitory. They were greeted at the door of the classroom with "Bonjour!" and then they found a seat. After learning some basic French phrases and food items, they were off on their first excursion to a French café.

Makayla pointed out the green awnings over the windows of a restaurant ahead. When they arrived, they heard "Bonjour!" and they all responded with "Bonjour!" They sat down and enjoyed some croissants in the soft candlelight of the dark interior. And then they talked for what seemed like hours.

As they trekked back to the dormitory with their counselor after their excursion to the café, Makayla tried to guess where in the world they would go next, "Do you think tomorrow we will be able to experience Morocco?"

"Oh, then we could have kabobs! That sounds wonderful!" Ava exclaimed. She was not disappointed. They did have kabobs before the end of the week, and they were just as delicious as Ava imagined.

Apply Vocabulary • *Skills Practice 1*

Name _____   Date _____

Compare and Contrast

> **FOCUS**
> - When writers **compare,** they tell how things, ideas, events, or characters are alike.
> - When writers **contrast,** they tell how things, ideas, events, or characters are different.

PRACTICE Read each sentence below. Decide if the sentence is showing a comparison or a contrast. Then, rewrite each sentence reflecting the other term.

1. Jack and Chloe are both in my class at school.

   _____

2. This movie is similar to the one we saw last week.

   _____

3. Olive and Madison would prefer drinking water to tea.

   _____

4. The mother signs "more" to her baby, and the baby also signs "more."

   _____

5. Both toddlers and teenagers are expected to attend the party.

   _____

6. We both go to a tutor after school on Tuesdays.

   _____

7. A bicycle has two wheels, in contrast to a tricycle, which has three wheels.

   _____

8. Daniel has a great sense of humor; however, he isn't able to tell a good joke.

   _____

Skills Practice 1 • Access Complex Text

UNIT 3 • Lesson 3 **195**

APPLY On the lines below, compare and contrast two things each about candlelight and a flashlight.

9. Compare: _____

_____

_____

_____

_____

_____

10. Contrast: _____

_____

_____

_____

_____

_____

Access Complex Text • *Skills Practice 1*

Narrative Writing

Think

Audience: Who will read your tall tale?

_____

Purpose: What is your reason for writing a tall tale?

_____

PREWRITING The setting of a story is where and when the events take place. Writers include vivid and descriptive details about their settings so a reader can clearly visualize, or "see with their mind's eye," the action in the story.

Think of the setting descriptions you have read in other narrative fiction stories. Then close your eyes, and imagine yourself in a setting from your own story. Provide words and phrases that answer the questions below to use in your story.

What do you see? _____

_____

What do you smell? _____

_____

What do you hear? _____

_____

What do you feel? _____

_____

What is the landscape like? _____

_____

Do any of the details described above help show when the story takes place?

_____

Revising

Use this checklist to revise your narrative writing.

☐ Does the story have a beginning?

☐ Does the story have a middle with rising action?

☐ Does the story have details about the setting?

☐ Does the story have a climax?

☐ Did you include enough humor and exaggeration?

☐ Is it clear that the story is a tall tale?

☐ Be sure all sentences have subject/verb agreement.

Editing/Proofreading

Use this checklist to correct mistakes in your narrative writing.

☐ Did you use proofreading symbols when editing?

☐ Did you check for mistakes in subject/verb agreement?

☐ Did you check that each sentence has an end mark?

☐ Did you check for mistakes in comma usage?

☐ Did you check the writing for misspelled words?

Publishing

Use this checklist to prepare your narrative writing for publishing.

☐ Write or type a neat copy of the narrative writing.

☐ Add a cover page with a title.

Suffixes *-ous, -eous, -ious;* Greek Root *onym*

FOCUS • Understanding and identifying **Greek roots** and their meanings can help you define and spell difficult and unfamiliar words.

onym = name

• The **suffixes** *-ous, -eous,* and *-ious* mean "possessing the qualities of." When they are added to base words, they form adjectives.

PRACTICE Add the suffix *-ous, -eous,* or *-ious* to the following base words to form spelling words. Write the spelling words on the lines.

Word List

1. acronym
2. ambitious
3. anonymous
4. continuous
5. courteous
6. eponym
7. glorious
8. gorgeous
9. hazardous
10. homonym
11. humorous
12. miscellaneous
13. mountainous
14. nutritious
15. obvious
16. righteous
17. spontaneous
18. studious
19. synonym
20. tedious

Challenge Words:

1. igneous
2. industrious
3. pseudonym

1. hazard _____

2. continue _____

3. miscellany _____

4. humor _____

5. tedium _____

6. industry _____

7. ambition _____

8. courtesy _____

9. spontaneity _____

10. glory _____

Fill in the missing root to form a spelling word.

11. syn_____

12. hom_____

13. ep_____

14. pseud_____

15. acr_____

16. an_____ous

APPLY Use the phrase to help you determine the spelling word that fits the description best, and write it on the line.

17. has the quality of being dull _____

18. has the quality of studying _____

19. fake name _____

20. same name _____

21. has the quality of danger _____

22. has the quality of politeness _____

23. has the quality of carrying on _____

24. has the quality of beauty _____

25. has the quality of mountains _____

26. has the quality of being healthful _____

27. has the quality of being unknown _____

28. has the quality of being apparent _____

29. has the quality of being correct _____

30. has the quality of being assorted _____

Subject/Verb Agreement

FOCUS
- **Subject/verb agreement** in a sentence means the verb agrees with the subject in number.

- The subject of a sentence is either singular or plural. The verb must agree with the subject in number.

  She **waits** at the table for her lunch.

  They **wait** at the table for their lunch.

- With a singular subject, add -s or -es to the regular verb. With a plural subject (or with the pronouns *you* or *I*), do not add -s or -es to the verb.

  Antonio **rides** the bus to school.

  Antonio and his sister **ride** the bus to school.

- A compound subject that uses the conjunction *and* takes a verb that agrees with the plural subject.

  Eli and Avery **hike** to the top of the mountain.

- A compound subject that uses the conjunction *or* takes a verb that agrees with the subject word that is closest to the verb.

  The gymnasts or their coach **takes** pictures.

PRACTICE Read each pair of sentences below. Place a check mark next to the sentence that has subject/verb agreement.

1. _____ I stays with my aunt on Saturday and my grandfather on Sunday.

   _____ I stay with my aunt on Saturday and my grandfather on Sunday.

2. _____ Lisbeth or her sisters throw a big party once a year.

   _____ Lisbeth or her sisters throws a big party once a year.

APPLY **Rewrite each sentence to correct mistakes in subject/ verb agreement.**

3. Paul go to the store while his friends stays home.

   _____

4. Everyone in our family love fruit.

   _____

5. Julius and Ryan plays in the tennis tournament.

   _____

6. The gas station down the street close early today.

   _____

7. The children or the teacher decorate the room for each holiday.

   _____

8. Tony sing beautifully.

   _____

9. Mia and Hannah always agrees about which show to watch.

   _____

10. Cheetahs runs faster than any other land animal.

    _____

11. Our turtles likes taking baths in water, but our gerbil prefer sand baths.

    _____

12. My sister move to a different apartment every year.

    _____

Grammar • _Skills Practice 1_

Prefixes *anti-, de-, super-,* and *trans-*

FOCUS The prefix *anti-* means "against." For example, when the prefix *anti-* is added to the word *social,* the new word *antisocial* means "against society" or "not friendly."

The prefix *de-* means "down" or "away." For example, the word *decrease* means "to go down in size," or in other words, "to make smaller."

The prefix *super-* means "above" or "beyond." For example, the word *supernatural* means "beyond natural."

The prefix *trans-* means "across" or "beyond." For example, the word *transcend* means "to climb beyond."

PRACTICE **Add the prefix *anti-, de-, super-,* or *trans-* to each base word below, and then write the new word's definition on the line. Use a dictionary if you need help.**

1. _____bacterial

    _____

2. _____grade

    _____

3. _____vise

    _____

4. _____pacific

    _____

5. _____part

    _____

6. _____cavity

    _____

APPLY Each word below uses the prefix *anti-, de-, super-,* or *trans-*. Use your knowledge of the base word or root's meaning to write an original sentence for each word.

7. transition _____

_____

8. antifreeze _____

_____

9. superstar _____

_____

10. antioxidant _____

_____

11. superimpose _____

_____

12. decide _____

_____

13. supernatural _____

_____

14. debris _____

_____

Vocabulary

FOCUS Review the selection vocabulary words from
"The House Baba Built."

abroad	engineer	scholar
betrayal	inseparable	shoots
captives	lolled	shrill
curfew	luscious	stoic
embassies	reprimanded	trance
		unison

PRACTICE Read each statement. Choose the vocabulary word that matches what is described and write it on the line.

1. Your parents give you a time to be home. <u>trance</u> or <u>curfew</u>? _____

2. You meet a person with advanced learning experiences.
   <u>scholar</u> or <u>shoots</u>? _____

3. You recite a poem together with your class at the same time.
   <u>unison</u> or <u>inseparable</u>? _____

4. You hear a high-pitched shrieking sound. <u>stoic</u> or <u>shrill</u>? _____

5. You sat by the pool talking with friends. <u>reprimanded</u> or <u>lolled</u>? _____

6. A friend told someone else your secret. <u>betrayal</u> or <u>trance</u>? _____

7. Your aunt is a person who designs structures, such as bridges.
   <u>engineer</u> or <u>scholar</u>? _____

8. You traveled outside of your country. <u>inseparable</u> or <u>abroad</u>? _____

9. Someone is awake but seems to be unaware of surroundings.

   trance or curfew? _____

10. Your uncle seems unwilling to show his emotions. shrill or stoic? _____

11. The characters in a movie are kept against their will by pirates.

    captives or shoots? _____

12. You transplant some young bamboo plants. shoots or scholars? _____

13. Your parents expressed disapproval with your action.

    reprimanded or lolled? _____

14. You stay near the offices of ambassadors to foreign countries.

    embassies or luscious? _____

15. You taste something that is full of flavor. luscious or stoic? _____

16. You cannot separate your feelings from the experience.

    inseparable or abroad? _____

APPLY Read each sentence. Answer each question by
explaining the definition of the underlined term in your own words.

17. The student is studying to be an engineer at the university. What will the

    student learn? _____

    _____

18. The athlete will travel abroad for international competition. Where might the

    athlete go? _____

    _____

Practice Vocabulary • *Skills Practice 1*

An Inseparable Sister

Because I am a teenager and my younger sister is still in elementary school, my parents often ask me to watch her. I would complain, but I know I would be reprimanded and my curfew might be an hour earlier, so I don't complain. Luckily for me, my sister has quite the imagination! So, on any given Saturday, I may be happily lolling on the sofa when my mother asks me to watch my little sister for a few hours. Soon my sister and I will be inseparable. She finds me almost at once.

"Good," she says, "I'm glad I found you. We have a situation."

"A situation?" I ask, waiting for her to explain what pretend situation she has for us to work out today.

"Yes, a situation," she says authoritatively. "Didn't you hear those shrill voices outside? Our neighbors are being held captive and we need to find out who betrayed them."

"Shrill voices? Captives? A betrayal? Oh, please tell me all the luscious details," I plead.

"Well, just one hour ago, I heard an argument outside," she said. "When I looked out the window, I saw someone, maybe a treasure hunter, grab our neighbor and say 'It's time to retrieve the secret treasure we stole. We will be inseparable until we find it.' And then, they started walking down the street."

"Really?" I ask, "Who would know that our neighbor has a hidden treasure? And who would betray our sweet neighbor?"

She looks at me, scrunching her face as if she is thinking hard, and then says, "I know just who to ask!" Then she whispers, "Now you pretend to be a professor, okay?"

"I can do that," I whisper back. I go over to the big desk and pull out a big book. I look as stoic and scholarly as I can as I pretend to read the book. My sister knocks and I look up, "Yes?" I ask.

"Good afternoon, Professor, I was wondering if you know someone with a treasure?" she asks.

"You are the second person to ask me today!" I share with her.

"Of course, I know someone with a treasure."

"Do you remember when I lived abroad and worked at the embassy?" I asked. My sister nodded, and I continued, "Well, when I worked for the ambassador, I met quite a few interesting characters and they all had fascinating stories that brought them to the embassy for help. One time I met an engineer who had built a bridge with a secret door that leads to a hidden treasure."

"Would you be able to identify this person if you saw this engineer again?" my sister asked stoically.

"I know many engineers, but I will never forget this engineer whose bridge hides a treasure," I say, "Especially an engineer that became our neighbor!"

"Oh! That is a twist I did not expect!" she says. "I know who betrayed that engineer." She pulls out a picture from a magazine and shows it to me. Then she asks, "Is this the other person who asked about the treasure today?"

"Yes, it is! How did you know?!" I respond with a shrillness that surprises both of us.

"I know things," she replies. "Now, do you know where this bridge is and can you find it?"

"Of course," I say, "I know things, too, and I never forget important things, like where a treasure is located or who created such a well-engineered hiding spot. Follow me." I tiptoe around the room, crouch behind some small bamboo shoots, and point to a bookshelf. "Look over there at the bridge. The door is hidden behind the structure."

"Maybe we can get there before our neighbor the engineer," she suggests as she looks around and then continues to the bookshelf. She pretends to open a door and smiles. She points and mouths the words, "The...treasure!" I tell her to grab it and get back to our hiding spot, and she does, dropping the treasure with me. Then, she jumps out and says, "Stop! You're under arrest for taking the secret treasure! We checked!" With that statement we pretend to grab our neighbor and friend and we run away as fast as we can. We hear the keys jiggling in the lock so we run and sit back onto the sofa in unison when our mother walks in.

"Have you been sitting there this whole time?" my mother reprimands. "You know your sister has quite the imagination!"

Copyright © McGraw-Hill Education

Apply Vocabulary • *Skills Practice 1*

Main Idea and Details

FOCUS Authors organize their writing into a main idea supported by details.

- A main idea should be clear and focused.
- A main idea should have supporting details. Details provide additional information about the main idea.

PRACTICE Read the paragraph below. Identify the main idea of each paragraph and write it on the line. Then, write two details from the paragraph that support the main idea.

Allie pictured herself traveling abroad all around the world. She imagined going to the top of the Eiffel Tower in Paris, France. She wanted to see the Great Pyramids in Egypt. She dreamed of swimming in the Great Barrier Reef in Australia. She hoped to walk across part of the Great Wall in China. Her travels would not be complete until she danced the tango in Argentina and the samba in Brazil.

1. Main Idea: _____

_____

2. Details: _____

_____

_____

_____

APPLY Write a main idea sentence for each set of details that is provided.

3. They started by planting a row of cabbage. In the next row, they planted zucchini. They added beets, radishes, and turnips in the last three rows.

_____

4. There was a duck pond game in one classroom. There was a ring toss in another classroom. In the gym, there was an obstacle course. There was face painting near the entrance of the carnival.

_____

5. She had charcoal pencils for drawing. She had pastels for blending color pictures. She had markers for making bold posters. She used tempera paint to create colorful landscapes.

_____

Write details for each of the main idea sentences.

6. My friends and I decorated our clubhouse to make it feel like home.

_____

_____

_____

7. We divide the household chores in our home.

_____

_____

_____

8. The singer performed songs in different styles.

_____

_____

_____

Narrative Writing

Think

Audience: Who will read your personal narrative?

_____

Purpose: What is your reason for writing a personal narrative?

_____

PREWRITING   **Think about experiences you have had that would make a good story. It might be something exciting that happened to you, but a great story can also come from a funny, sad, or unusual experience. For each word below, write a short description of an experience you had that was . . .**

strange. _____

_____

humorous. _____

_____

exciting. _____

_____

educational. _____

_____

Revising

Use this checklist to revise your narrative writing.

- [ ] Does the story have a beginning, middle, climax, and end?

- [ ] Is it clear that the story is a personal narrative?

- [ ] Is it written in first-person?

- [ ] Does the story include dialogue?

- [ ] Does the dialogue sound natural?

- [ ] Are there places where additional descriptions could be added?

- [ ] Are there words that can be replaced with better, more precise words?

Editing/Proofreading

Use this checklist to correct mistakes in your narrative writing.

- [ ] Did you use proofreading symbols when editing?

- [ ] Have you checked for run-ons and sentence fragments?

- [ ] Is the dialogue punctuated correctly?

- [ ] Did you check the writing for misspelled words?

- [ ] Did you check the writing for mistakes in capitalization?

Publishing

Use this checklist to prepare your narrative writing for publishing.

- [ ] Write or type a neat copy of your personal narrative.

- [ ] Use a multimedia source when publishing or presenting the writing.

Prefixes *anti-*, *de-*, *super-*, and *trans-*

FOCUS Many words contain prefixes, and knowing the meanings of prefixes can help you understand the meanings of new or difficult words.
- The **prefix *anti-*** means "against."
- The **prefix *de-*** means "down" or "away."
- The **prefix *super-*** means "above" or "beyond."
- The **prefix *trans-*** means "across" or "beyond."

PRACTICE Add the prefix *anti-*, *de-*, *super-*, or *trans-* to the following base words and word parts to form spelling words.

Word List		Challenge Words
1. antibiotic	**11.** superficial	**1.** deactivate
2. antibodies	**12.** superhuman	**2.** superintendent
3. antiseptic	**13.** supersede	**3.** translucent
4. antisocial	**14.** superstar	
5. antivirus	**15.** supervise	
6. decay	**16.** transaction	
7. decline	**17.** transatlantic	
8. deduct	**18.** transformation	
9. dejected	**19.** translate	
10. deport	**20.** transport	

1. _____sede

2. _____late

3. _____jected

4. _____social

5. _____vise

6. _____cay

7. _____star

8. _____duct

9. _____atlantic

10. _____port

11. _____ficial

12. _____port

Copyright © McGraw-Hill Education

13. _____biotic   **17.** _____bodies

14. _____action   **18.** _____cline

15. _____virus   **19.** _____septic

16. _____formation   **20.** _____human

APPLY If the word is spelled incorrectly, write the correct spelling on the line. If the word is spelled correctly, write *Correct*.

21. supercede _____

22. antisepic _____

23. transacion _____

24. superficial _____

25. antevirus _____

26. transatlantic _____

27. dijected _____

28. antesocial _____

29. declign _____

30. translate _____

31. supervies _____

32. deactevate _____

33. antibodies _____

34. deducked _____

Run-Ons and Sentence Fragments

FOCUS
- A **complete sentence** must have a subject and a predicate. A complete sentence expresses a complete thought.

  Mr. Newcastle's horses sleep in the barn.

- A **sentence fragment** is a group of words that do not express a complete thought. A sentence fragment is missing a subject or a predicate. A dependent clause that stands alone is also a segment fragment. It is missing the word or words that the clause modifies.
  The cracked glass in the windowpane. (*no predicate*)
  Left early without telling anyone. (*no subject*)
  Before the ice on the pond thaws. (*dependent clause standing alone*)

- A **run-on sentence** has more than one clause and is missing the correct punctuation or conjunction.
  We missed our flight to Houston another flight leaves in two hours.

PRACTICE Identify each sentence below as *R* if it is a run-on, *F* if it is a sentence fragment, or *C* if it is a complete sentence.

1. _____ Until the trumpeter swam arrived at the zoo.

2. _____ My phone needs to be recharged I left the cord at home.

3. _____ The green van driving across the bridge.

4. _____ The soup in the fridge is starting to smell funny.

5. _____ The sun sinks slowly the shadows grow longer.

6. _____ A letter to the president.

APPLY Rewrite the sentences to correct each run-on or sentence fragment.

7. I entered my painting in an art show it won second prize.

_____

_____

8. If the mosquitoes are not too bad tonight.

_____

_____

9. My report about the Great Depression.

_____

_____

10. Brooke finished reading *Hatchet* she did not care for it.

_____

_____

11. Gavin's team made it to the tournament they won the last six games in a row.

_____

_____

12. Always cares for his aunt's plants when she is away.

_____

_____

13. Saskia wants to live on a farm someday she might be a vet in a big city.

_____

_____

14. Whenever the weather is warm enough.

_____

_____

Greek Root *bio*; Latin Roots *aud, rupt*

FOCUS Identifying and understanding Greek and Latin roots can help you define unfamiliar words. When you know the meaning of a root, you can determine the meanings of many words that contain that root.

The Greek root *bio* means "life." For example, the word biography means "the story of a person's life written by someone else."

The Latin root *aud* means "hear." For example, the word audio means "relating to sound." The Latin root *rupt* means "break." For example, the word erupt means "to break out" or "explode."

PRACTICE Read each word. Circle the root *bio, aud,* or *rupt* in each one. Then write the definition of the word on the line.

1. audience

_____

2. interrupt

_____

3. bionic

_____

4. rupture

_____

5. biology

_____

6. audible

_____

APPLY Choose a word from the box to complete each sentence. Each word contains the Greek root *bio,* the Latin root *aud,* or the Latin root *rupt.* Write the word on the line.

abruptly	antibiotic	auditions	auditorium
biodegradable	biographical	eruption	interrupt

7. We were prescribed a(n) _____ to fight the skin infection.

8. The children's soccer game in the backyard ended _____ when one child twisted his ankle.

9. Water bottles and cans are not _____, but they can be recycled.

10. Please do not _____ me when I'm speaking on the phone.

11. _____ for the school play will take place Thursday after school.

12. The choir will be performing a spring concert tonight in the school _____.

13. The sports program gives _____ information about each of the players.

14. You can see the _____ of the geyser several times a day.

Word Analysis • *Skills Practice 1*

Vocabulary

FOCUS Review the selection vocabulary words from "Just 17 Syllables!"

charming	melancholy
clearing	pondered
expressway	regularly
fiddled	shogun
gradually	verse
insurance	welled

PRACTICE Read each sentence. Think about the meaning of the underlined word or words. Write the vocabulary word on the line that is similar in meaning.

1. I sang the first <u>section of the song</u> and then everyone joined in singing the chorus.

_____

2. As the day went on, it <u>little by little</u> became warmer.

_____

3. We drove the car onto the <u>wide road with several lanes</u> to travel faster.

_____

4. Bashō was a <u>Japanese military leader from long ago</u> who wrote poetry.

_____

5. Tears <u>gathered at the surface</u> in her eyes as she recalled her deep disappointment.

_____

6. The <u>attractive</u> little house sat at the edge of the woods.

_____

7. The family had <u>protection against loss or damage</u> for their home.

_____

8. The boy <u>aimlessly played</u> with the zipper on his jacket.

_____

9. Look at the deer standing in the <u>open piece of land free from trees</u> near the stream.

_____

10. The girl <u>thought carefully about</u> her options for a research topic.

_____

11. We went for walks in the neighborhood <u>again and again at about the same time</u>.

_____

12. He felt <u>a deep sadness</u> when he thought about losing his family pictures due to a flood.

_____

APPLY **Read each question. Think about the meaning of the underlined vocabulary word. Write your answer on the line.**

13. What might cause someone to feel <u>melancholy</u>? _____

14. What would you see on an <u>expressway</u>? _____

15. What is something that you have <u>pondered</u>? _____

16. What is something you do <u>regularly</u>? _____

17. What are some things that <u>gradually</u> get bigger? _____

18. What might make someone seem <u>charming</u>? _____

Practice Vocabulary • *Skills Practice 1*

Poetry Jam

Anthony loved to read poetry, and he read poetry with some regularity. He read all types of poetry—free verse, rhyming, and even haiku. He loved how the words created pictures in his mind. He enjoyed pondering the deeper meanings of the verses he read. He was constantly surprised by the many subjects of the poetry—one day he would read poems about nature and the next about ancient Japanese shoguns.

In addition to reading poetry, Anthony loved to write poetry. He wrote regularly and had notebooks full of poetry. The subjects of his poetry ranged from describing a deer in a clearing to telling the story of an ancient hero or battle. He constantly wrote ideas for new poems, whether he was at the dentist's office or riding in a car on the expressway. Even the walls of Anthony's room were covered with poetry verses!

One day, tragedy struck Anthony and his family. While they were away from home, their small, charming house burned to the ground, along with all their possessions. Although the family had insurance on the house, Anthony's poetry was not easily replaced. He did not keep extra copies of his poems elsewhere. As Anthony thought about all the years of poetry that filled his room, tears welled in his eyes.

A deep melancholy settled into Anthony, and he stopped reading the poetry he loved. He stopped writing the poetry that once filled his room. He had a hard time just finding meaning in his life. He pondered the purpose of writing all those poems to have them gone in an instant. His friends tried to cheer Anthony up, bringing him poetry books and empty notebooks, but nothing seemed to work.

As the weeks and months went by, life gradually began to get back to normal. The family received the insurance money to buy a new home, and they moved to a charming house in town. This home was located across the street from the local library. The library seemed to call to Anthony at once, and before long he made regular stops there. The librarians all knew him by name, and soon they became well-versed in all Anthony's favorite poets and poetry.

Once Anthony started reading poetry again with regularity, he began to write poetry again. He started with one verse, and then added another.

Anthony's love of poetry spread to everyone who knew him. He would charmingly recite a new poem he had read to friends who were feeling melancholy. He gradually began to share poems he wrote with the librarians. And they, in turn, began thinking of ways to include poetry in the programming at the library. They began a poetry club that met regularly to ponder, discuss, and recite poems. They created special classes to help people write poetry and recite poetry with more expression.

In the spring, the librarians told Anthony that the library would be hosting a Poetry Jam. At this event, people would share poetry they memorized or wrote. They could have practice sessions before the event so everyone could improve their delivery of the their poems. They would love for Anthony to begin the event. He could write a poem just for the event—one that expressed his love of poetry.

Anthony went home, pulled out an empty notebook page, and began to ponder what would be a good way to begin the poetry event. He fiddled with his pen, trying to think of the best way to express his love of poetry. This was a tough assignment, and he was not sure he could think of the best way to share that love because he had too many ideas. So, he wrote just a verse or two about one topic, and then a verse or two about another.

He reread the verses he wrote, and he began to see a gradual progression of ideas. He started to see how all his ideas were connected, and he worked on tying them together with additional words and descriptions. He felt like a painter of words, creating different moods with the colorful words he chose. When the poem was finished, he read it over and over, memorizing it.

Anthony attended the classes at the library that focused on presenting poetry to an audience. He practiced making his voice rise and fall. He practiced projecting his voice so the person in the back of the room could hear. He remembered feelings of joy and melancholy and tried to express those as he recited the words. After weeks of practicing regularly, he was ready.

On the night of the Poetry Jam, Anthony recited his poem with such emotion and expression, the librarians welled with pride.

Apply Vocabulary • *Skills Practice 1*

Fact and Opinion

FOCUS Good writers use both facts and opinions in their writing. A good reader can tell one from the other.
- **Facts** are details that can be proven true or false.
- **Opinions** are what people think. They cannot be proven true or false.

PRACTICE Read each sentence below and tell whether it is a fact or an opinion.

1. Haiku is the easiest poetry to write. _____

2. Haiku is poetry with three lines. _____

3. Bashō was known for writing haiku poetry. _____

4. Bashō wrote beautiful and interesting haikus. _____

5. Japan is an island nation in Asia. _____

6. Shoguns were military rulers in Japan before the revolution of 1867–1868.
   _____

7. Shoguns were great leaders in Japan. _____

8. It is important to get insurance for your home. _____

9. Car insurance will protect against the loss or damage of a car. _____

10. The minimum speed on the expressway is 45 miles per hour. _____

APPLY Write one fact and one opinion you have about each topic below. Use complete sentences.

11. haiku

Fact: _____

Opinion: _____

12. Japan

Fact: _____

Opinion: _____

13. sports

Fact: _____

Opinion: _____

14. music

Fact: _____

Opinion: _____

Narrative Writing

Think

Audience: Who will read your fantasy?

_____]

Purpose: What is your reason for writing a fantasy?

_____]

PREWRITING **Use the pyramid diagram below to visually structure your plot. Remember to start at the base, work up to the climax, and then go back down the pyramid where the conflict is resolved.**

Climax

Rising Action   **Falling Action**

Beginning   **End**

_____   _____
(conflict introduced)   **(conflict resolved)**

Revising

Use this checklist to revise your narrative writing.

- [ ] Does the story have a beginning, middle, and end?
- [ ] Does the story include an element that makes it a fantasy?
- [ ] Does the writing have a variety of sentence types?
- [ ] Do the events happen in a logical order?
- [ ] Does the writing include sensory details that create a mood?
- [ ] Does the writing use time and order words?
- [ ] Does the story have a climax, or turning point?

Editing/Proofreading

Use this checklist to correct mistakes in your narrative writing.

- [ ] Did you use proofreading symbols when editing?
- [ ] Are compound and complex sentences punctuated correctly?
- [ ] Did you check the writing for correct use of irregular nouns and verbs?
- [ ] Did you check the writing for misspelled words?
- [ ] Did you check the writing for mistakes in subject/verb agreement?

Publishing

Use this checklist to prepare your narrative writing for publishing.

- [ ] Write or type a neat copy of the narrative writing.
- [ ] Give the story a title, and include a visual element, like an illustration.

Greek Root *bio*; Latin Roots *aud, rupt*

FOCUS Understanding and identifying Greek and Latin roots and their meanings can help you define and spell difficult and unfamiliar words. Here are the roots in the spelling words and their meanings:
Greek root *bio* = "life;" **Latin root *aud*** = "hear;"
Latin root *rupt* = "break"

PRACTICE Fill in the missing root to form a spelling word.

Word List		Challenge Words
1. abrupt	11. bankrupt	1. neurobiology
2. amphibious	12. biodiversity	2. symbiotic
3. audience	13. biography	3. uninterrupted
4. audiobook	14. biology	
5. audiology	15. disrupt	
6. audiovisual	16. eruption	
7. audit	17. inaudible	
8. auditorium	18. interruption	
9. auditory	19. microbiologist	
10. autobiography	20. rupture	

1. _____itorium

2. inter _____ion

3. micro _____logist

4. e _____ion

5. _____iology

6. _____ure

7. dis_____

8. ab_____

9. in_____ible

10. _____ience

11. auto_____graphy

12. _____diversity

13. _____iovisual

14. _____logy

15. _____it

16. amphi_____us

17. _____graphy

18. _____iobook

19. _____itory

20. bank_____

APPLY On the line, write the spelling word that is best represented by the definition. Use a dictionary if you need help.

21. study of hearing _____

22. a place for hearing _____

23. a sudden outbreak _____

24. someone who studies microscopic life _____

25. a group who hears _____

26. quality of varied life forms _____

27. written work about someone's life _____

28. written work about one's own life _____

29. break apart _____

30. book made for hearing _____

Circle the correctly spelled words.

31. symbiotic   symbotic

32. rupcher   rupture

33. audeovizuel   audiovisual

34. abrupped   abrupt

35. auditory   odditory

36. amphibious   amfibeous

37. intraruption   interruption

38. bankrupped   bankrupt

39. audit   oddit

40. bialigy   biology

Irregular Nouns and Irregular Verbs

FOCUS
- Most **regular plurals** are formed by adding -s or -es to the singular noun, sometimes with a small change to singular noun.

park	park**s**
kiss	kiss**es**
berry	berr**ies**
wolf	wol**ves**

- **Irregular nouns** do not follow this rule. They change in a different way, or they do not change at all.

tooth	**teeth**
mouse	**mice**
deer	**deer**

- **Regular singular verbs** have -s or -es added to the base verb, while a regular plural verb is the base verb with nothing added.

He **walks**.   They **walk**.

- **Irregular verbs** use different words for the singular and plural forms. The verbs *be, have,* and *do* are irregular verbs.

Milo **is** here.	His sisters **are** here.
The boat **has** a leak.	The boats **have** leaks.
She **does** well.	They **do** well.

PRACTICE For each singular word below, write its plural form on the line.

1. goose _____

2. sheep _____

3. hero _____

4. turkey _____

5. child _____

6. person _____

7. fish _____

8. bench _____

APPLY Complete each sentence below by writing the correct form of the verb in parentheses on the line.

9. Will _____ going to the beach this year for vacation. (be)

10. Kylie's dog _____ not like going to the vet. (do)

11. I _____ a new bike because my old one was too small. (have)

12. Caleb and Dylan _____ to give a presentation in class today. (have)

13. Elephants _____ the heaviest land mammals on Earth. (be)

14. Your notebooks _____ need to be put away during the test. (do)

15. Jonas _____ not remember where he put his tennis shoes. (do)

Write a sentence that contains the plural form of each word in parentheses.

16. (man) _____

_____

17. (foot) _____

_____

18. (moose) _____

_____

19. (cactus) _____

_____

20. (species) _____

_____

The Very Best Sport

"Watch out!" yelled Grant. It was too late. The soccer ball spun right into the side of Cliff's head.

"Oh . . . sorry," Cliff yelled back absentmindedly.

"What's going on?" Grant asked in an irritated voice. "You need to pay more attention. We need a lot more practice before we play in this weekend's game."

Cliff and Grant lived on the island of Barbados in the eastern Caribbean Sea. They were playing soccer, one of the island's most popular sports for students. Cliff and Grant's team was doing well and was favored to win in the upcoming game, but Cliff's heart was not in it.

Since he had starting playing sports as a little boy, Cliff had always felt like he was being pushed in a direction he did not want to go. He had not liked cricket; the first sport he had attempted. Cricket is the national sport of Barbados, and almost everyone on the island plays. Cliff, however, had found the game, which involved batting a ball and running between two stumps called wickets, quite boring.

When Cliff was a little older and his parents detected his lack of enthusiasm for cricket, they had suggested soccer. Millions of people around the world love the game, and Cliff was a good athlete, so it was natural for him to give it a try. Unfortunately for Cliff, he was good at it. It all came naturally to him, but it just did not excite him. Even now, when his team was headed for a championship, he could not keep his mind on it. Instead, Cliff dreamed of water, waves, and the big, warm winds of the Caribbean.

After practice Cliff ran straight home and grabbed his windsurf board, or sailboard. Windsurfing is a popular sport for natives and visitors to Barbados. Most students in Cliff's school, however, preferred the team sports of soccer, basketball, and, of course, cricket. But windsurfing was the sport for Cliff.

After school the following day, Cliff stopped off at the local surfboard shop. He liked checking out all the new windsurfing equipment, even if he could not afford it. He could always dream about it, and maybe someday he would start winning competitions and earn enough money to actually buy all this stuff. And then he would compete in the Olympics!

As Cliff was about to leave, something on the wall caught his eye. A brightly colored brochure announced an upcoming windsurfer competition. A small prize would be awarded to the first-, second-, and third-place finishers. Cliff was ecstatic. He knew he was ready for a competition—and this could be his big break. He grabbed the brochure and started reading the details. "Oh, no," Cliff said aloud, "the competition is this Saturday, and the big soccer game is this Saturday too. Now what am I going to do?"

At first Cliff felt as if he could not really talk about this with his parents. How could they understand his dilemma when they really wanted him to become a big soccer star or the next cricket sensation? "Well that's never going to happen," laughed Cliff, "so I might as well tell them the truth."

After dinner that night Cliff told his parents about his dream of becoming a champion windsurfer, how he had absolutely no desire to play soccer or cricket, and about the windsurfing competition on Saturday. Cliff was surprised; his parents seemed only a little disappointed. His mom, of course, expressed her concern about all the tricks he was doing on the sailboard, but Cliff assured her he was training properly. What they seemed most disappointed about was the problem of the soccer game on Saturday.

"Do you really want to let your team down, Cliff?" his father asked, looking directly into Cliff's eyes. "Think about Grant and your other friends. They've been practicing hard, and this is important to them."

"But the competition is important to me!" Cliff replied. As he said the words, however, he knew what he had to do. He had committed to the soccer team and the school. The windsurfing competition would have to wait.

"I'll play in the game and support my friends," Cliff said. "But just wait until the next windsurfing competition. I'm going to show Barbados what I can do! And finally I'm going to compete at the very best sport there is!"

Spice Up Your Day

What is your favorite food? Do you eat a special snack after school? Can you name some of the popular foods you and your friends eat? These foods may be common in some homes, but families in other parts of the world enjoy different types of foods for their meals.

India is a country in southern Asia. It is home to more than one billion people. Many Indians do not believe in eating animals. They do not eat animals for religious reasons or for ethical reasons (they do not feel it is the right thing to do). People who do not eat animals are called vegetarians.

You may be asking yourself, "What do vegetarians in India eat?" They actually have many food choices. In fact, Indian diets are becoming more popular in the United States as well.

On a typical day in many parts of India, children rise to the smells of their parents cooking a breakfast of potatoes, onions, yogurt, fresh fruit, tea, and coffee. Many spices are used in Indian cooking. A popular breakfast dish is made with rice, lentils, and spices. Lentils are the seeds of a plant similar to peas and beans. Other popular breakfast foods include rice pancakes filled with vegetables, rice noodles, and cakes made with rice and peas and served with bananas.

As children in India open their lunch bags, they find a bread called *naan*. Naan is soft, round, and flat. It is filled with many types of vegetables and sometimes cheese or yogurt to make a sandwich. People in India also might eat fresh salads, fruit, spicy potatoes, vegetable soups, and rice for lunch.

After a long day at school or at work, Indians enjoy the aroma of spices coming from their homes. Before hitting the books, Indian children might have a snack. One favorite is crispy rice loops. No, this is not a breakfast cereal. Crispy rice loops are made from rice flour that is deep-fried into the shape of loops. Many people eat them with tea. As with other Indian recipes, many snack recipes have been passed down through the generations.

But it is not a good idea to fill up on snacks. Many wonderful recipes await, and dinner is ready! A typical Indian dinner might include various kinds of dumplings. Salads made from carrots, cucumbers, pineapple, and mango are often on the menu as well.

Once again, rice, lentils, and vegetables make up many of the dinner recipes. Of course, they are blended with many different spices, some of them very hot! You may have heard of chili powder. It is also popular in many recipes in the United States. This is a common spice in Indian cooking along with some you may not have heard of, such as cumin and the curry leaf. A popular side dish in America is cottage cheese. Cottage cheese is also popular in India. It is used in many dishes mixed with green peppers, black pepper, and spinach.

As in many different countries, the end of a day would not be complete without a sweet treat. Desserts in India include rice, carrots, and nut puddings. Many Indian desserts are made using nuts, coconut, pumpkin, and fruits such as pineapple and mango. One of the most popular desserts in India is a type of carrot pudding. It is made with nuts and other dried fruit.

These dishes are accompanied by various drinks. Two popular drinks in India are coffee and tea. However, Indian drinks are usually flavored with spices. Chilled mangos and nuts make good shakes. One Indian drink that has made its way to the United States is chai. *Chai* is the Hindi word for "tea." Chai is a spiced milk tea and is more popular in India than coffee. The next time you visit a coffee shop, try the chai!

Vegetarians can be found in every country. Most recipes can be changed to meet their needs. But in no other nation is being a vegetarian as much a part of life as in India. People around the globe can thank Indian cooks for inspiring some of the most delicious and healthful recipes in the world.

Fluency • *Skills Practice 1*

Vocabulary

FOCUS Review the selection vocabulary words from "My Librarian Is a Camel."

archipelago	isolated
capabilities	nomadic
caravan	promote
consists	refugee
devour	refurbished
economical	solar

PRACTICE Complete each sentence with a selection vocabulary word. Each vocabulary word should be used once.

1. The _____ lights work by storing energy from the sun.

2. We will travel in a _____ so we can stay close to each other as we drive to the cabin.

3. When I love a story, I will _____ the book quickly.

4. My uncle _____ the old table our great-grandfather built.

5. The ferry stopped at four islands of the _____.

6. The _____ tribe moved depending on the seasons and available resources.

7. The mobile phone has many different _____, including taking pictures, sending texts, and calling.

8. The _____ traveled far to flee the war that broke out.

9. It was difficult to reach the _____ mountain village because no one had made roads.

10. This salad _____ of spinach, strawberries, almonds, and a light dressing.

11. To _____ good dental health, the dentist is providing free toothbrushes.

12. The _____ choice on the menu is the daily special.

APPLY Read each sentence. Answer each question by explaining the definition of the underlined term in your own words.

13. You are traveling in a caravan to the big game. What are you doing?

_____

14. The economical car does not have many features. What does that mean?

_____

15. A BLT sandwich consists of bacon, lettuce, and tomato. What does that mean?

_____

16. The dancing toy worked by solar energy. What is happening?

_____

17. The auto collector refurbished an old car. What did she do?

_____

18. We tried not to devour our lunch, even though we were hungry. What does that mean?

_____

Practice Vocabulary • *Skills Practice 1*

Devoured Books

Melanie was full of questions and devoured books in search of the answers to those questions. Her book diet consisted of both nonfiction and fiction books related to a topic to get a full understanding. She had a strong capability to visualize as she read. She had so many questions about a topic, that sometimes the librarians would lead her to whole sections of the library.

Melanie wondered, "What would it be like to live nomadically in Africa?" So, she began to look up books about nomadic life. She read realistic fiction about modern nomads, and she especially enjoyed reading about the caravans traveling by camel. She could imagine the way the camels walked, the heat of the desert, and the cool shade of the tent. She then read historical fiction about ancient nomadic tribes in other parts of the world.

After reading about nomadic life, Melanie wondered, "What would it be like to live isolated from others?" This was a little harder to find on her own in the library, so she asked the librarians for help. They directed her to many fictional stories of survival in isolating conditions. She was amazed by the characters' capabilities of finding ways to stay alert and strong to overcome such loneliness.

Once she finished reading all she could find about living alone and in isolation, she began to wonder, "How could I power something if I lived alone?" She went to the library and began devouring books about all types of power: solar power, wind power, and electricity. As she read more, she learned an economical way of providing heat in some isolated communities involved heating dry animal manure!

The next topic for her inquiring mind was life on an archipelago. She wondered "How connected are the people who live on neighboring islands of archipelagos?" She read nonfiction stories about island life and learned about different archipelagos around the world. She imagined living on an archipelago, feeling the wind from the sea, the smell of salt water, the sounds of the waves lapping the shore. And she wondered, "Why would anyone leave such a beautiful place?"

Then Melanie began to learn more about refugees in the world. She devoured news articles and books that described the refugee experience. She imagined their fear and uncertainty as they traveled far from home.

Melanie began to imagine her life as an adult. She wanted to promote reading and help others find books, like the librarians helped her. Only, she wanted a place where people could buy books economically, so they could read them again and again. She wanted a place where people could meet and share books and stories. She wanted a place that used renewable energy resources, so maybe her place would be powered by solar panels. She wanted a place that would be welcoming and inviting.

As Melanie grew older, she continued to think about what her book store would look like. She imagined all the different places she visited in her mind while she devouringly read. Maybe her store could look like a nomadic caravan of books. Maybe her store could look like life on an archipelago. As she was walking through town, she found the perfect spot in the suburbs, several miles from the closest library. It was an old restaurant that would need to be refurbished, however it would be work well.

Melanie refurbished the old restaurant, so that it was now a book store with shelves and shelves of books. She kept a small section of the restaurant so people would have a place to read and have a cup of tea or coffee while they discussed books. She began promoting her book store and events she would hold. She scheduled authors to come visit so they could promote their books. She set up book clubs that consisted of neighbors interested in similar genres and topics.

On opening day, Melanie welcomed everyone into her book store. People came from all over town to see what was available and what programs she might offer. The neighbors of the store were amazed at how she was able to refurbish the restaurant for this new purpose. They were excited about the programs and economical options for books. The store was humming with people sharing books and stories, just as she imagined.

Soon, Melanie had a regular set of customers. They would come to greet her, talk books, and ask many questions. One of Melanie's favorite customers was a young boy who had a question-asking capability similar to her own. She looked forward to directing him to a section of the store to find answers. She smiled as he devoured book after book.

Apply Vocabulary • *Skills Practice 1*

Classify and Categorize

FOCUS • To **classify** is to identify the similarities that objects, characters, or events have in common with each other, and then group them by their similarities.

• To **categorize** is to organize the objects, characters, or events into groups, or categories.

PRACTICE On the lines below, building items are categorized into tools and supplies. Classify the items listed in the word box by placing them into the appropriate category.

hammer	bolt	nail	saw
wood	screwdriver	wrench	screw

1. **Tools**

   _____

   _____

   _____

   _____

2. **Supplies**

   _____

   _____

   _____

   _____

APPLY **Classify the emotions listed in the box by placing them into their appropriate categories.**

melancholy	joy	sorrow	fury	glumness	rage
cheerfulness	bliss	irritation	wrath	contentment	misery

3. Happy

_____

_____

_____

_____

4. Sad

_____

_____

_____

_____

5. Angry

_____

_____

_____

_____

Graphic Organizer Resources

Cause and Effect

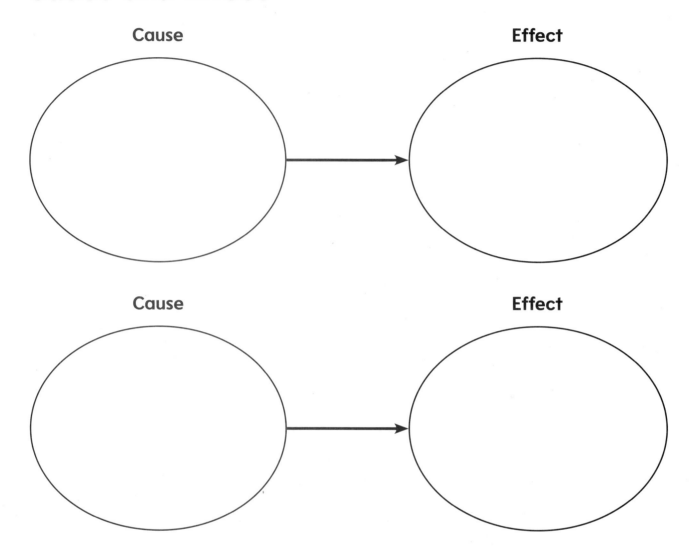

Cause

Effect

Cause

Effect

Compare and Contrast

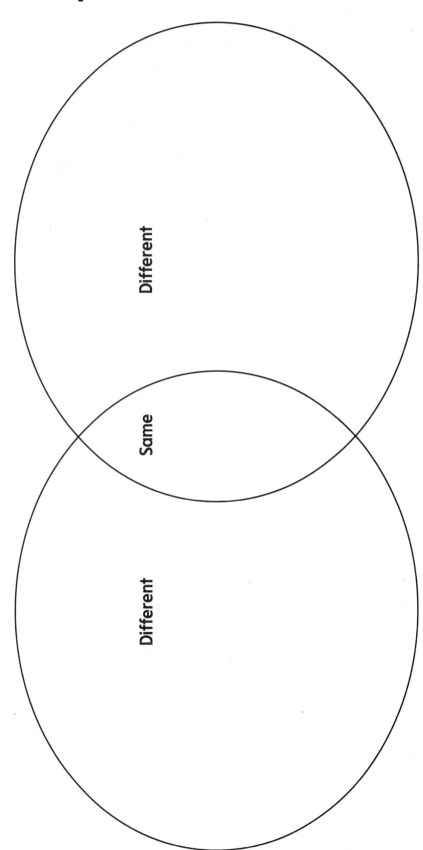

Fact and Opinion

OPINION	FACT

Main Idea and Details

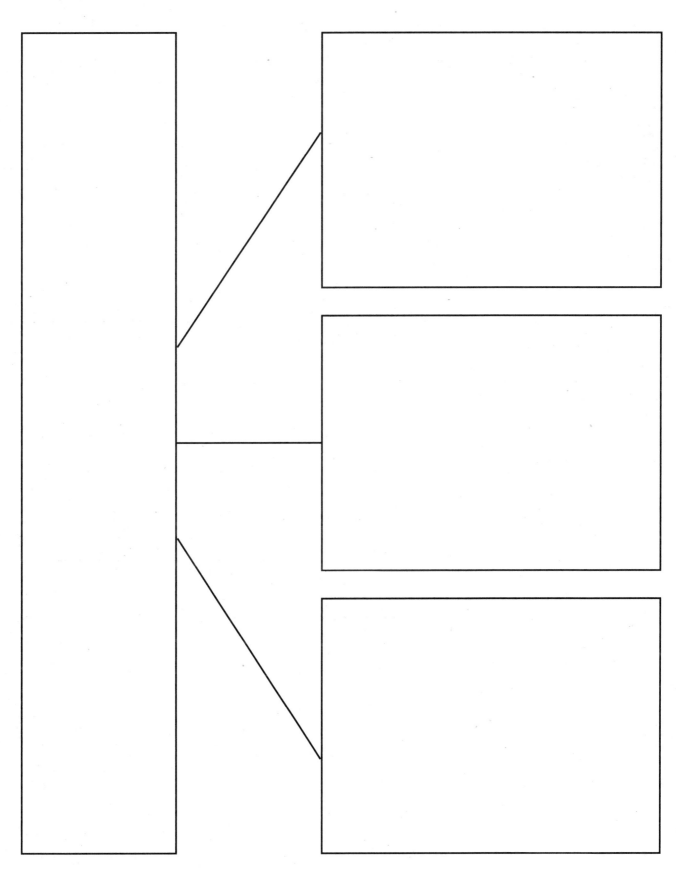

Making Inferences

Inference

=

Prior Knowledge

+

Clue

Sequence

First

┌───┐
│   │
│   │
│   │
│   │
└───┘

Next

┌───┐
│   │
│   │
│   │
│   │
└───┘

Last

┌───┐
│   │
│   │
│   │
│   │
└───┘

Clues/Problems/Wonderings

C	P	W

Know/Want to Know/Learned

K	W	L

Word Map

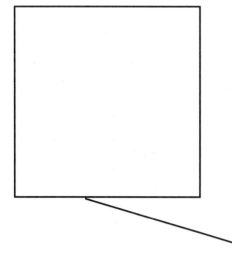

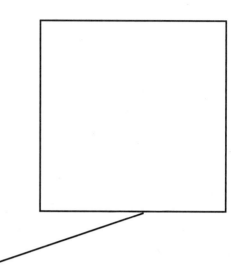

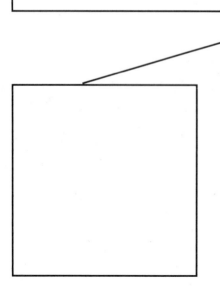

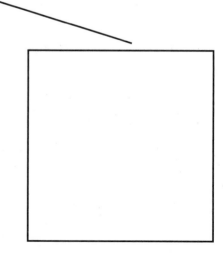

Name _____ Date _____

Plot

Solution:

```
┌─────────────────────────────────────┐
│                                      │
│                                      │
│                                      │
│                                      │
└─────────────────────────────────────┘
                   ▲
                   │
```

Climax

```
┌─────────────────────────────────────┐
│                                      │
│                                      │
│                                      │
│                                      │
└─────────────────────────────────────┘
                   ▲
                   │
```

Problem:

```
┌─────────────────────────────────────┐
│                                      │
│                                      │
│                                      │
│                                      │
└─────────────────────────────────────┘
```

4-Column Chart

TIDE

T	**Topic Sentence—Tell what you are explaining.**
ID	**Important Details—3 or more.** **First Detail**
	Second Detail
	Third Detail
E	**Ending—Wrap it up right.**

TREE

T	**Topic Sentence—Tell what you believe.**
R First Reason **E**	**Reasons—3 or more. Explain each reason further.** **Reason:** **Explanation:**
Second Reason	**Reason:** **Explanation:**
Third Reason	**Reason:** **Explanation:**
E	**Ending—Wrap it up right.**

WWW-H2-W2

W	**W**ho are the characters in the story?
W	**W**hen does the story take place?
W	**W**here does the story take place?
H	**H**ow do the characters react at different points in the story?
H	**H**ow does the story end?
W	**W**hat does the main character want to do?
W	**W**hat happens in the story?

Name _____ Date _____

Idea Web

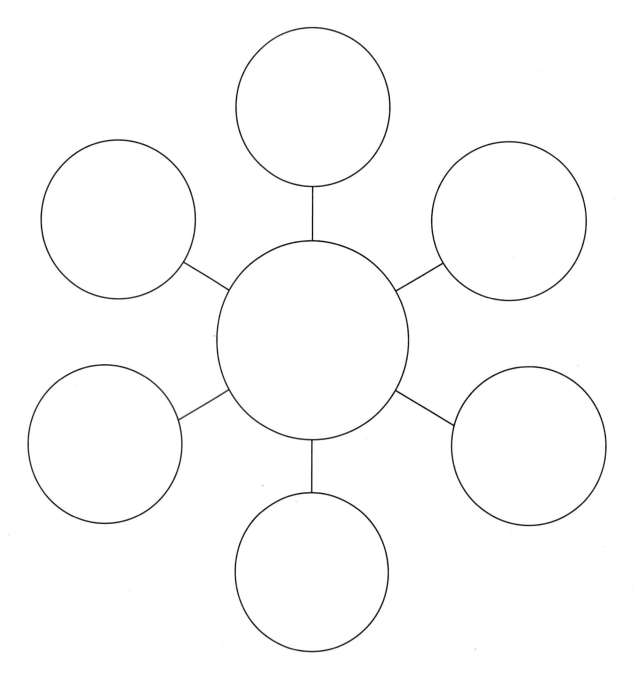

256